If a Mountain Lion Could Sing

Also by Red Pine/Bill Porter

Travel Writings (as Bill Porter)

South of the Yangtze: Travels Through the Heart of China

Finding Them Gone: Visiting China's Poets of the Past

The Silk Road: Taking the Bus to Pakistan

South of the Clouds: Travels in Southwest China

Yellow River Odyssey

Zen Baggage: A Pilgrimage to China

Road to Heaven: Encounters with Chinese Hermits

Chinese Poetry

Choosing to Be Simple: Collected Poems of Tao Yuanming

A Shaman's Lament: Two Poems by Qu Yuan

Cathay Revisited

Written in Exile: The Poetry of Liu Tsung-yuan

The Mountain Poems of Stonehouse

Guide to Capturing a Plum Blossom by Sung Po-jen

In Such Hard Times: The Poetry of Wei Ying-wu

The Collected Songs of Cold Mountain

Chinese Poetry Anthologies

Dancing with the Dead: The Essential Red Pine Translations

Poems of the Masters: China's Classic Anthology of T'ang and Sung Dynasty Verse

The Clouds Should Know Me by Now: Buddhist Poet Monks of China (with Michael O'Connor)

Buddhist, Zen, and Taoist Texts

Zen Roots: The First Thousand Years

Stonehouse's Poems for Zen Monks

Trusting the Mind: Zen Epigrams

A Day in the Life: The Empty Bowl and Diamond Sutras

The Lankavatara Sutra: Translation and Commentary

Lao-tzu's Taoteching: With Selected Commentaries from the Past 2,000 Years

The Platform Sutra: The Zen Teaching of Hui-neng

The Heart Sutra: The Womb of Buddhas

The Diamond Sutra: The Perfection of Wisdom

The Zen Works of Stonehouse: Poems and Talks of a Fourteenth-Century Chinese Hermit

The Zen Teaching of Bodhidharma

P'u Ming's Oxherding Pictures and Verses

If a Mountain Lion Could Sing

The Lyric Poems of Xin Qiji

Red Pine

Copper Canyon Press
PORT TOWNSEND, WASHINGTON

Printed in the United States of America

Cover image: Front gate of the Xin Qiji Memorial Hall in his hometown of Jinan, Shandong province. Photo by Li Xin.

Frontispiece: Portrait of Xin Qiji by unknown artist.

Copper Canyon Press is in residence at Fort Worden State Park in Port Townsend, Washington, under the auspices of Centrum. Centrum is a gathering place for artists and creative thinkers from around the world, students of all ages and backgrounds, and audiences seeking extraordinary cultural enrichment.

LIBRARY OF CONGRESS CATALOGING-IN-PUBLICATION DATA
Names: Xin, Qiji, 1140–1207, author. | Red Pine, 1943– translator.
Title: If a mountain lion could sing : the lyric poems of Xin Qiji / Xin Qiji ; translated by Red Pine.
Description: Port Townsend, Washington : Copper Canyon Press, 2025. | Includes bibliographical references and index. | Parallel text in Chinese and English on facing pages. | Summary: "A collection of poems by Xin Qiji, translated by Red Pine who is also known as Bill Porter"—Provided by publisher.
Identifiers: LCCN 2024043271 (print) | LCCN 2024043272 (ebook) | ISBN 9781556596865 (paperback) | ISBN 9781619323100 (epub)
Subjects: LCSH: Xin, Qiji, 1140–1207—Translations into English. | LCGFT: Poetry.
Classification: LCC PL2680 .I4 2025 (print) | LCC PL2680 (ebook) | DDC 895.11/42—dc23/eng/20250131
LC record available at https://lccn.loc.gov/2024043271
LC ebook record available at https://lccn.loc.gov/2024043272

9 8 7 6 5 4 3 2 FIRST PRINTING

COPPER CANYON PRESS
Post Office Box 271
Port Townsend, Washington 98368
www.coppercanyonpress.org

Contents

If a Mountain Lion Could Sing

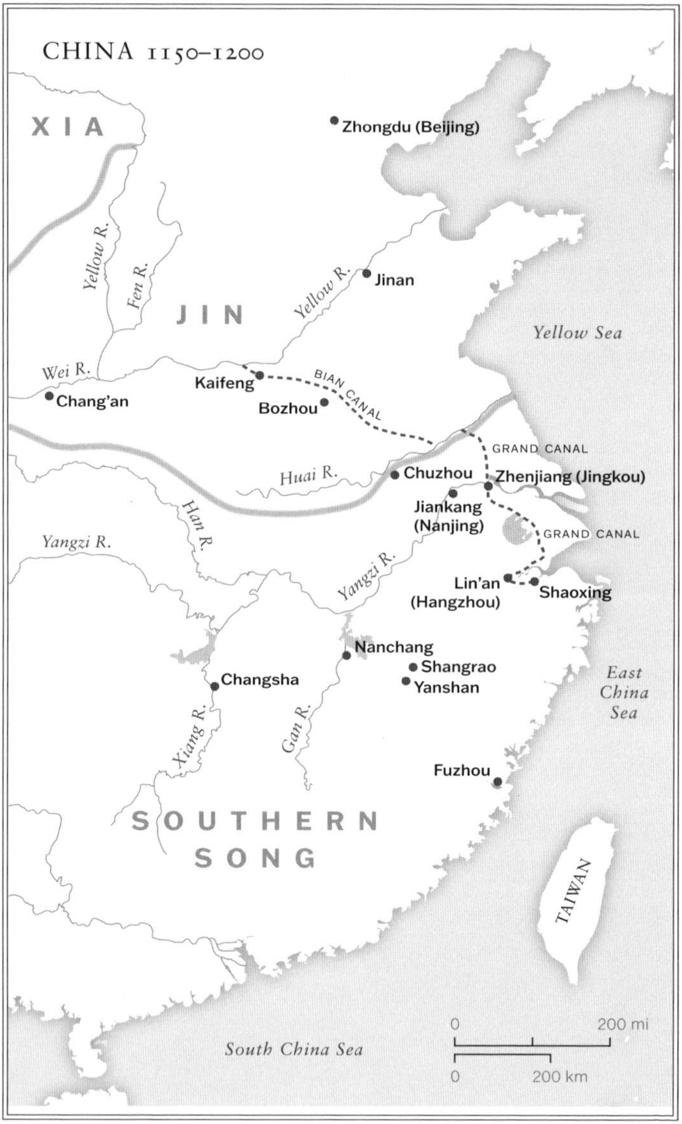

CHINA 1150–1200
XIA
Zhongdu (Beijing)
Yellow R.
Fen R.
JIN
Yellow R.
Jinan
Yellow Sea
Wei R.
Chang'an
Kaifeng
BIAN CANAL
Bozhou
GRAND CANAL
Huai R.
Chuzhou
Zhenjiang (Jingkou)
Han R.
Jiankang
(Nanjing)
GRAND CANAL
Yangzi R.
Yangzi R.
Lin'an
(Hangzhou)
Shaoxing
Nanchang
Shangrao
Yanshan
Changsha
East
China
Sea
Xiang R.
Gan R.
Fuzhou
SOUTHERN
SONG
TAIWAN
South China Sea
0
200 mi
0
200 km

Translator's Preface

For the past 2,500 years, China has been home to some of the world's greatest poets. The man whose work fills this book was one of them. And yet he was not like any of them. Mention his name to a Chinese person and watch their chest rise in admiration. It's not just his poetry; it's who he was. And it's not just who he was; it's his poetry, his lyric poetry. No one sang a poem the way Xin Qiji 辛棄疾* sang a poem. Chinese literary critics came up with a term for it: *hao-fang* 豪放—"unrestrained" or "with heroic abandon." Su Dongpo 蘇東坡 (d. 1101) was the first major poet in China to explore this genre. Xin Qiji made it his home: letting his heart write poems to melodies that have long since been forgotten. Although the melodies are gone, his words still resonate with the spirit for which his compatriots have cherished them ever since. Of the forty Chinese poets whose homes and graves I visited in *Finding Them Gone,* Xin Qiji was the one who stopped me, as they say, in my tracks. I had never paid much attention to his poetry. It was written to music, and I wasn't surprised so little of it had been translated. He was only on my list because my friend Paul Hansen told me Xin Qiji was his favorite poet. And so I visited the memorial hall where Xin's home once stood. When I read the poem on the entrance ticket (#39), I suddenly understood why Paul felt the way he did. It was different, but it wasn't hard to understand. In fact, it was barely

*Also romanized Hsin Ch'i-chi, his name is pronounced Sin Chee-gee.

a poem—which was its point. And at least for me, falling in love doesn't take that much.

My new dance partner was born in 1140. In the decades prior to his birth, northern China was invaded by the armies of a seminomadic people from northern Manchuria known as the Jurchens 女真. The Jurchens had previously helped the Han Chinese defeat a tribal confederation from southern Manchuria known as the Khitans 契丹. Following their victory over the Khitans, the Jurchen armies didn't return home. They were suddenly at the gates of the Song capital of Kaifeng 開封. In January of 1127, they sacked the city and took the emperor prisoner. Everyone who could fled south. After crossing the Yangzi, the surviving members of the royal family set up a new capital, first in Jiankang 建康 (Nanjing 南京), then in Lin'an 臨安 (Hangzhou 杭州). To reflect this relocation, they began referring to the dynasty's previous reign period as the Northern Song 北宋 and the new one as the Southern Song 南宋. Their former territories in the north, meanwhile, became part of the Jin 金 dynasty of the Jurchens.

Xin Qiji was born in the Jurchen territory of northern China, just outside the city of Jinan 濟南, the capital of what is now the dragon-head province of Shandong. His father died when he was eight, and he was raised by his grandfather, Xin Zan 辛贊. The owner of considerable property, his grandfather had remained in the north. He even became a mid-ranking official in the Jin government—the Jurchens were only too happy to let someone else run the realm they now controlled. At the time of his son's death, Xin Zan was serving as magistrate of the ancient city of Bozhou 亳州, three hundred kilometers southwest of Jinan, and he arranged for his grandson to join him there. He enrolled Xin Qiji in a school operated by a famous local poet named Liu Zhan 劉瞻. Although we have no stories about Xin Qiji's journey to becoming the most famous poet of his time, this would have been when it began. Liu was an admirer of the poetry and lifestyle of the farmer-recluse Tao Yuanming 陶淵明 (d. 427), and his admiration rubbed off on the young boy, who later listed Yuanming as one of his role models. Xin's grandfather also became a role model. Despite his high status under the Jurchens, Xin Zan was hardly an obedient servant. He often told his grandson about the time the Han Chinese ruled the land where he was born and urged him to dedicate himself to reclaiming it for his descendants. It was with this in mind that he changed the boy's name from You'an 幼安 "peaceful child" to Qiji 棄疾 "panacea."

Xin was a precocious student. At the age of fifteen, and again when he was eighteen, he traveled to the Jin capital of Zhongdu 中都, in what is now Beijing, to take the examinations that, if passed, would open the door to a career as an official. Before each trip, his grandfather told him to note the disposition of Jurchen forces. Raising a peaceful child was not what the old man had in mind. He groomed the boy to be a rebel. Not all Xin's friends received such encouragement. One of his classmates at Liu's school was Dang Huaiying 黨懷英, who later rose to the highest ranks of the Jin bureaucracy, becoming minister of education. As it happened, Xin failed the examinations both times, but I have to wonder what he would have done had he passed. As he grew up, his grandfather saw to it that Xin mastered skills such as horse riding and swordsmanship—even military strategy. Certainly, Bozhou would have been the perfect place to learn such things. It was the home of one of China's greatest warriors, Cao Cao 曹操 (d. 220), as well as the home of the legendary heroine Hua Mulan 花木蘭 (ca. fifth century), who disguised herself as a man so she could take her father's place in the compulsory draft.

In 1158, Xin's grandfather received a new appointment as magistrate of Kaifeng—one of the highest positions available to a Han Chinese person under the Jurchens. Although the Jurchens had destroyed the former Song capital, they rebuilt the city and made it their southern capital. The city was too important not to rebuild. It was located at the conjunction of the Yellow River and the Bian Canal 汴渠 that linked it to the Huai River 淮河, which formed the border between the Jin and Song realms. Unfortunately, Xin Zan died soon after assuming his new post, sometime between 1158 and 1160. My guess is that it was no later than the beginning of 1159. Otherwise, Xin Qiji would not have had time to complete the period of mourning before he could strap on a sword and fulfill his grandfather's wishes.

At the beginning of 1161, Jin armies launched new attacks on Song forces along the Huai, and local uprisings occurred in the Jinan region. Sensing this was the time he had been waiting for, the twenty-two-year-old grandson raised a force of two thousand men, among them a monk named Yiduan 義端. After taking part in local skirmishes, Xin joined his force with a larger one of over ten thousand men headed by Geng Jing 耿京. One night while they were camped and getting ready to attack the Jurchens, Yiduan snuck into Geng's tent, stole the seal used to authenticate documents, and fled to the enemy camp. When Geng learned of this, he was furious and had Xin Qiji brought before him. He ordered Xin executed on the spot for introducing him to the traitorous monk. Xin asked Geng to grant him three days. If he did not return with the seal, he would willingly offer up his head. Impressed with Xin's sincerity, Geng agreed. Xin then gathered fifty of his best men, charged into the enemy camp, found Yiduan, and brought back the seal, along with the monk's head. That is why when Chinese people hear Xin Qiji's name, they react differently than when they hear the names of other poets.

Later that year, Xin suggested to Geng Jing that they coordinate their efforts with those of the Song court. Geng agreed, and in the first month of 1162 Xin traveled to the Southern Song capital in Jiankang. Although Emperor Gaozong 高宗 granted Xin an audience, he was reluctant to commit his own forces to fight the Jurchens. He did agree, however, to support Geng's independent army. Unfortunately, just as Xin left Jiankang, he learned that Geng had been assassinated by their fellow insurrectionist Zhang Anguo 張安國. As soon as he returned north, Xin once again led a small band on horseback into the Jurchen camp where Zhang had taken refuge. Once again, he found his quarry. This time he didn't cut off his head. He brought Zhang back to Jiankang so the emperor could witness the execution.

During the years that followed, Xin became a popular figure at the Southern Song court. Both Emperor Gaozong and his successor, Xiaozong 孝宗, admired Xin. Still, both men followed a policy of appeasement toward the Jurchens—it was cheaper than fighting them. Xin Qiji's entreaties to retake their lost lands in the north went unheeded. He was politely ignored and was kept busy going from one midlevel post to another in the region known as Jiangnan 江南 (South of the Yangzi), which formed the heartland of the Southern Song domain. It was during this period that Xin started writing poems, or at least sharing them. Given their startling beauty, and given the care he later displayed in preserving what he wrote, he must have been writing poems for some time. If so, they were lost while he was engaged in fighting the Jurchens. Writing poems, though, does not seem to have occupied much of Xin's attention at the posts where he served. He had other things on his mind. He was still a warrior at heart, waiting for the emperor to send him into battle. It was not until he was relieved of the burden of government service that poetry became his life. Before then, he did what he could wherever he was stationed to train the soldiers attached to his post in fighting skills and military strategy. Eventually, news of what he had been doing aroused the suspicions of his enemies at court, where not everyone appreciated his patriotic fervor. They accused him of organizing his own military force. In 1181, at the age of forty-two, he was forced into an early retirement.

Instead of letting this ruin his life, Xin followed the ancient Chinese tradition of turning retirement into a new career, one in which he devoted himself to self-cultivation, to visiting friends and scenic sights, and, finally, to writing poems, especially poems set to music. The place Xin Qiji chose to do this was the town of Shangrao 上饒—over three hundred kilometers, or "a thousand *li*," as he often wrote, southwest of the Southern Song capital of Lin'an. Xin had spent time in this region earlier as judicial, and later military, commissioner of Jiangxi 江西, the province in which Shangrao was located. And he had become friends with such famous residents of the area as Chen Liang 陳亮 and Zhu Xi 朱熹 (d. 1200), the leading neo-Confucian thinkers of his time, both of whom also advocated fighting the Jurchens and reclaiming the Song homelands—to the consternation of the court.

What was unusual about Xin's retreat to the countryside was

the residence in which he decided to spend his retirement years. It wasn't like the cottage in which Du Fu 杜甫 (d. 770) took refuge in Chengdu or the countryside shrine Wei Yingwu 韋應物 (d. 791) moved into outside Chang'an 長安. When Xin came south, so did the family's money. The series of residences that he developed—which included the odd "hut" for those times when he wanted to be alone and unencumbered—were essentially estates. The first of these was on the shore of Daihu 帶湖 (Ribbon Lake)—a former stream that had been dammed to form a ribbon-shaped body of water—just outside Shangrao's north gate. Xin must have sensed what was on the horizon. He began construction on the buildings in 1178, three years before he was forced to retire. The philosopher Zhu Xi once happened to visit Xin's Daihu Lake home when the poet wasn't there and wrote that he had never seen such a place. Eight years later, Xin bought an even larger parcel of land—by some accounts, over three hundred acres—thirty kilometers southwest of Shangrao and just south of the town of Yanshan 鉛山. The land included some houses next to a spring, and soon after buying it Xin began recreating a simpler version of what he built at Daihu Lake. He named his new residence after the spring: Piaoquan 瓢泉 (Gourd Spring). Whether at Daihu or Piaoquan, Xin Qiji spent the last thirty years of his life as a retired gentleman of considerable means, entertaining and visiting friends and writing poetry that is still memorized by every schoolchild in China.

Interruptions to Xin's bucolic life occurred from 1192 to 1194, when he was asked to take up a minor post on the coast in Fuzhou 福州 due to the death of the incumbent, and again from 1203 to 1204, when he was asked to come to the aid of the prime minister, Han Tuozhou 韓侂胄. Han had taken control of the government and had resumed military campaigns against the Jurchens. When Han's efforts failed, he blamed Xin. Han had to blame someone. The Jurchens asked for Han's head as the price for peace. Although Xin returned home, it wasn't for long. A few months later, in the spring of 1205, the emperor asked him to take over as magistrate of the strategic city of Zhenjiang (Jingkou), as it guarded the entrance to the southern section of the Grand Canal and direct access to the capital. After less than a year, Xin decided he had had enough. Also, he was ill. He returned to Gourd Spring in the fall of 1205 and died there two years later, in the fall of 1207.

Of the 735 poems Xin left behind, 75 percent were written within the thirty-kilometer-wide circle bounded by Daihu Lake and Piaoquan Spring. I can't help smiling at the thought of how the animosity of Xin's enemies at court has provided the world with such a treasure. Among the jewels he left us, some are in the traditional *shi* 詩 style, in which all the lines have the same number of words, or characters, arranged in a limited set of tonal patterns. Xin's collected works include just over a hundred such verses. But the genre in which he had no peer was the *ci* 詞, or lyric, style, in which the length of lines keeps changing to match melodies with over eight hundred tonal patterns. Reflecting their musical origins, lyric poems were usually composed in two stanzas, with their length dependent on the melody but their syntactic and thematic relationship dependent on the poet. The difference between these two genres was like that between classical music and jazz. Lyric poems were a fusion of the poet's emotions with the setting they described. Spontaneity was their hallmark. They were also meant to entertain. It's no coincidence that Xin was as famous for his essays on music as he was for those on military strategy. An image that has often come to mind while translating Xin's lyric poems is of someone picking a flower bud and opening its petals, one line at a time.

Altogether, Xin left 629 lyric poems, far more than any other poet whose work has come down to us. Not only did he write more lyric poems, he wrote them to more melodies* and themes than anyone else. Although the melodies haven't survived—no one wrote them down—the poems have, and not by accident. Such was his fame when he was alive, Xin's first collection was published in a printed edition in 1188, when he was only forty-nine! This was followed by a second, a third, even a fourth collection, which was published just before his death. In compiling a selection of these poems, I have tried to order my choices chronologically, so readers might get a sense of what was going on in his life as well as his development as a poet. Xin was a great help in this regard, as he often noted the date after the tune title or the circumstances of his composition. Also a great help were Chinese commentators who have noted usages or references in the poems that are datable. Those poems for which a date would have just been a guess, I have placed at the end of my selection.

Lyric poems didn't have titles based on their subject or occasion. They were simply referred to by their first line and also by the name of the tune to which they were written. Since the name of the tune rarely, if ever, had anything to do with the poem, I have titled the poems by their first line. Readers can find the names of the tunes in the notes to each poem and also at the back of this book, where I

*Although little has been done to restore the original melodies on which lyric poems were based, a good explanation of the relation between the music and lyrics can be found in the book by Shi Yidui 施議對 titled 詞與音樂關係研究.

have added an index of the tune titles in English and Chinese, identifying which poems were composed to them.

As for the title of this book, in June of 2023, I had an opportunity to visit the places where Xin Qiji wrote most of the poems collected here. My final stop was his grave. I had been there a decade earlier, while visiting the homes and graves of thirty-nine other Chinese poets of the distant past. This time I only had one poet on my itinerary, and with me were several local scholars who helped me locate the places around Shangrao and Yanshan that Xin wrote about. And joining us were two dozen of their friends.

Since my previous visit, the dirt trail to his grave had been replaced by one with polished stone steps—a considerable upgrade for such a remote place. It was raining, and suddenly I slipped. I fell flat on my back and hit my head on the steps. Everyone gasped. I lay there, surprised to find myself looking up at the rain. It was an oddly relaxing, if unusual, position to find myself in. If I had been alone, I might have lain there for a while enjoying the rain on my face. Seeing a forest of faces staring down at me, I caught my breath and got back up—much to the relief of all those who had spent the day accompanying me—and, to my surprise, I was without any apparent injury. I proceeded up the last steps to the grave, with people holding on to both my arms to make sure I didn't fall again. After we had all gathered around Xin Qiji's grave, I poured a local 100-proof liquor (named in his honor) on the tombstone and read the last poem he wrote: "Comparing Worthies and Fools" (number 105). I then recited my English translation, bowed, and left.

A month later, back at home and getting ready to send the first draft of these translations to the publisher, I had a dream. A mountain lion jumped onto my back. When I raised my left hand to knock it off, it bit my arm and wouldn't let go. I then swatted the mountain lion's flank a few times with my right hand, and it finally jumped onto the ground. It looked up at me and said, "I'm going to sing." And that was what it did, as we both made our way down a forested hillside and into a mountain village that looked like it was out of a Song-dynasty painting. The dream then wandered off, as dreams always do. When I woke in the morning, the dream was as vivid as if it had just taken place. I concluded Xin Qiji had paid me a visit, and I had heard him sing, his voice. That is where the title of this collection came from. I know, there aren't any mountain lions in China, and it was just a dream. It was, though, my dream, and this was as good a way as any of thanking Xin Qiji for keeping me company while I was translating his poems, and for protecting me while I was following him around to the places where he wrote and sang them such a long time ago.

Red Pine
Summer 2024
Port Townsend

The Poems

1 春已歸來

春已歸來，看美人頭上，嫋嫋春幡。
無端風雨，未肯收盡餘寒。
年時燕子，料今宵夢到西園。
渾未辦黄柑薦酒，更傳青韭堆盤。

卻笑東風從此，便薰梅染柳，更沒些閑。
閑時又來鏡裏，轉變朱顏。
清愁不斷，問何人會解連環。
生怕見花開花落，朝來塞雁先還。

Written to the tune "Han Palace Spring" in the first month of 1163, when Xin Qiji was twenty-four, with the note: "First day of spring" 立春日. This is Xin Qiji's earliest known poem, lyric or otherwise. It was written in the strategic town of Zhenjiang across the Yangzi from Yangzhou and what was left of the northern half of the Grand Canal. The town guarded the entrance to the Grand Canal's southern half. He first arrived there the previous year at the head of a force of ten thousand men who had joined him in rebelling against the Jurchens. His men then became part of the Southern Song army, and following an audience with Xiaozong, who succeeded Gaozong that summer, Xin returned to Zhenjiang. Soon afterward, he married the daughter of Fan Bangyan 范邦彦 and set up a household near his in-laws—to which he often returned between assignments. "West Garden" refers to one with that name at the imperial palace in the former Song capital of Kaifeng, now occupied by the Jurchens, who made it their southern capital. Citrus wine and plates of such strong-smelling things as onions and leeks were among the offerings prepared for one's ancestors on the first day of spring. The east wind is the wind of spring in China, while the west wind is the wind of fall. Jade disks were sometimes carved with one disk joined to another as a symbol of an unbreakable bond. Here, they represent Xin Qiji's bonds to his homeland, of which he is painfully reminded. Though newly arrived, he already envies the geese heading back north.

1 Spring Is Back Already

Spring is back already
I can see it in women's hair
in their spiraling new ribbons
and yet the thoughtless wind and rain
aren't ready for the cold to end
last year's swallows
surely are dreaming in West Garden tonight
and yet I haven't prepared the sacrificial citrus wine
much less the plate of leeks

I have to laugh as the east wind begins
perfuming plum trees and dyeing willows green
and doesn't rest
and when it does and I look in a mirror
my rosy cheeks won't be the same
and my sorrows won't be gone
does anyone know how to separate linked disks of jade
how I hate to see flowers bloom and fall
geese heading north today before me

2 家住江南

家住江南，又過了清明寒食。
花徑裏一番風雨，一番狼藉。
紅粉暗隨流水去，園林漸覺清陰密。
算年年落盡刺桐花，寒無力。

庭院靜，空相憶。
無說處，閒愁極。
怕流鶯乳燕，得知消息。
尺素如今何處也，彩雲依舊無蹤跡。
謾教人羞去上層樓，平蕪碧。

Written to the tune "Whole River Red" in 1164, with the note: "Late spring" 暮春. Xin received his first assignment in 1164 to Jiangyin 江陰, a bit farther down the Yangzi from Zhenjiang, as a notary, or signatory official, whose role was to countersign documents. Purification Day was originally (in Confucius's time) the third day of the third lunar month. It was later given a solar date—namely, the day after Cold Food Day, which occurs 105 days after the winter solstice. Purification Day is now celebrated as Grave Sweeping Day. Climbing somewhere high was part of many celebrations in ancient China. Xin Qiji recounted how his grandfather often led him to the top of a tower so he could look out at the lands his ancestors had lost to the Jurchens. "The grasslands" refers to those of northern China, where Xin perfected his skills on horseback.

2 Since Moving South of the Yangzi

Since moving south of the Yangzi
I have once more spent Cold Food and Purification Days
in gusts of wind and rain on a flower-lined path
amid a profusion
of pink and red silently flowing past
in the orchard's ever-darkening cool shade
I have noticed every year once the paulownia flowers fall
the cold weather is done

In the stillness of the courtyard
I think of someone in vain
what can I say
about an utterly useless sadness
I fear the orioles and swallows
might have some news
the whereabouts of a silken letter
promising clouds as usual vanish without a trace
don't tell me to forget about climbing towers
or how green the grasslands are

3 少年痛飲

少年痛飲，憶向吳江醒。
明月團團高樹影，十里水沉煙冷。

大都一點宮黃，人間直恁芬芳。
怕是秋天風露，染教世界都香。

Written to the tune "Peace and Purity" around 1166, with the note: "Recalling admiring a cassia tree on the Wu River" 憶吳江賞木樨—a river near Suzhou. Near the end of 1164, Xin was made comptroller general of the Guangde Army 廣德軍. Although it was headquartered in Jiankang, its units were spread throughout the lower reaches of the Yangzi, which gave Xin the opportunity to explore the region. The assignment lasted until 1167. The Chinese see a cassia tree on the moon. The color favored in palace attire was a pale, gosling yellow, similar to that of the tiny, fragrant flowers of the cassia, which transformed the world that night on the Wu River. I can't help smiling at the thought of Xin, in his mid-twenties, reflecting on something that happened in his younger days.

3 I Loved to Drink When I Was Young

I loved to drink when I was young
I recall sobering up on the Wu River
the image of the great tree on the perfectly full moon
ten miles of cold perfumed water

Due to nothing but its pale palace-yellow
everyone suddenly smelled sweet
as if windblown dew in the autumn sky
had imbued the whole world with the scent

4 風月小齋模畫舫

風月小齋模畫舫，綠窗朱戶江湖樣。
酒是短橈歌是槳。
和情放，醉鄉穩到無風浪。

自有拍浮千斛釀，從教日蒲桃漲。
門外獨醒人也訪。
同俯仰，賞心卻在鴟夷上。

Written to the tune "Fisherman's Pride" around 1166, while Xin Qiji was briefly in the Huzhou area, with the note: "Building a houseboat at Huzhou headquarters" 湖州幕管作舫室. Such boats were popular in the lake region of the lower Yangzi, especially on Huzhou's Lake Taihu 太湖, one of the largest freshwater lakes in China. Although grape wine appeared in China during the Neolithic, it wasn't popular until a sweeter version arrived as a luxury good via the Silk Road during the Han dynasty. The poet Li Bai 李白 was a fan. Chinese wineskins, like Spanish botas, were made of goat leather and used for carrying wine while traveling.

4 An Open-Air Study on a Painted Houseboat

An open-air study on a painted houseboat
a red door and green windows floating-life style
with wine for our paddle and song for our oar
we let our feelings go
and reached that drunken state where wind and waves disappear

I have swum in a thousand vats of mash
spent day after day getting drunk on grape wine
sobering up when a guest arrives
looking each other up and down
happy to see a wineskin

5 翡翠樓前芳草路

翡翠樓前芳草路，寶馬墜鞭暫駐。
最是周郎顧，尊前幾度歌聲誤。

望斷碧雲空日暮，流水桃源何處。
聞道春歸去，更無人管飄紅雨。

Written to the tune "Regretting Your Departure" around 1167—most likely in Nanjing, where Xin was posted as one of the city's two comptrollers general this year—with the note: "Spring thoughts" 春思. The scene in the first stanza is that of the road through a town's entertainment section—kingfisher blue was a color women favored for their eyebrows, often using the bird's actual feathers. Zhou Yu was famous for knowing when a musician played the wrong note. Blue clouds are those still visible after the sun goes down. "Peach Blossom Spring" 桃花源 refers to the land lost in time, written about by Tao Yuanming and discovered by following peach petals in a stream to their source. In Xin Qiji's poem, their falling petals mark the end of spring.

5 Before a Kingfisher-Blue Inn on a Perfumed Road

Before a kingfisher-blue inn on a perfumed road
a jeweled horse and whip suddenly stopped
Zhou Yu surely would have noticed
when someone who's been drinking got a tune wrong

I wonder where blue clouds go after sunset
or where Peach Blossom Spring's water comes from
once people hear springtime is over
no one pays attention to floating petals in the rain

6 我來吊古

我來吊古，上危樓，贏得閑愁千斛。
虎踞龍蟠何處是，只有興亡滿目。
柳外斜陽，水邊歸鳥，隴上吹喬木。
片帆西去，一聲誰噴霜竹。

卻憶安石風流，東山歲晚，淚落哀箏曲。
兒輩功名都付與，長日惟消棋局。
寶鏡難尋，碧雲將暮，誰勸杯中淥。
江頭風怒，朝來波浪翻屋。

Written to the tune "Recalling a Pretty Girl" in 1168 in Nanjing, with the note: "For Regent Shi Zhidao, climbing Jiankang's Shangxin Pavilion" 登建康賞心亭呈史留守致道. This tower still stands, overlooking the Qinhuai River 秦淮河 as it flows west through Nanjing (Jiankang) and into the Yangzi. The tower looks down upon the area where the nobility and well-to-do lived during the Six Dynasties (220–589) as well as during the Southern Song (1127–1279), when Nanjing served as the subsidiary capital and location of much of the administration. Shi Zhidao (Zhengzhi 正志) represented the emperor in Nanjing when the ruler was at court in Hangzhou. Xie An 謝安 (d. 385) left his hermitage on East Mountain 東山 south of Shaoxing 紹興 for the capital (Nanjing) to rescue the Eastern Jin dynasty from northern invaders. He was one of Xin Qiji's heroes. According to an old story, a fisherman once found a mirror that could reveal what was in a person's heart. Unfortunately, he dropped it in the Qinhuai River, and it was never found again. Xin had begun serving in Jiankang at the end of the previous year as one of several comptrollers general, responsible for countersigning documents.

6 I Came Here to Mourn the Past

I came here to mourn the past
to the top of this tower
with enough wine to dispel my sorrows
as for where tigers and dragons are hiding
I only see the usual changes of fortune
beyond the willows and slanting light
birds returning to the river
great trees moaning along the dike
boats sailing west
someone playing a flute

I think back to Xie An's manner
his last years on East Mountain
crying when he heard a sad tune
having placed his hopes in his children
he played chess all day
true mirrors are hard to come by
for blue clouds at sunset
who lifts a cup of wine
the wind on the river was wild
the waves this morning washed houses away

7 千里渥洼種

千里渥洼種，名動帝王家。
金鑾當日奏草，落筆萬龍蛇。
帶得無邊春下，等待江山都老，教看鬢方鴉。
莫管錢流地，且擬醉黃花。

喚雙成，歌弄玉，舞綠華。
一觴為飲千歲，江海吸流霞。
聞道清都帝所，要換銀河仙浪，西北洗胡沙。
回首日邊去，雲裏認飛車。

Written to the tune "Water Music Song" in the fall of 1168 in Nanjing, with the note: "Birthday wishes for Transport Deputy Chief Zhao Jie'an" 壽趙漕介庵. Zhao was a member of the royal family and was serving in Nanjing—where Xin was also serving. Xin likens the entertainers Zhao invited to three famous immortals. The Celestial River is the Milky Way, and "Huns" here refers to the Jurchens. Xin is enthused by the prospect that the court might be changing its policy of appeasing their enemies and might soon reclaim its lost lands. Newly arrived in the south, Xin can't help listening to rumors. Since Zhao was about to leave for court in Lin'an (Hangzhou), the poem ends with a vision of his means of transport.

7 Like a Thousand-Mile Steed

Like a thousand-mile steed
your reputation moved the throne
when you submitted your draft to the palace
your calligraphy resembled dragons at play
since you brought us a world of spring
we've been waiting for it to fade
yet your temples are still black
unconcerned with what it might cost
you proposed a chrysanthemum party

You summoned Paired Perfection
such singers as Polished Jade
a dancer the like of Green Splendor
and wine that would make us immortals
we drank a river of liquid sunset
and heard in the royal precincts
they're planning to reroute the Celestial River
to scour the northern sands of the Huns
turning our heads toward the sun
we'll be looking for your chariot in the clouds

8 儂是嶔崎可笑人

儂是嶔崎可笑人，不妨開口笑時頻。
有人一笑坐生春。

歌欲顰時還淺笑，醉逢笑處卻輕顰。
宜顰宜笑越精神。

Written to the tune "Washing Silk in the River" in 1169 in Nanjing, with the note: "To Ziwen's attendant, Xiao-xiao ['smile-smile']" 贈子文侍人，名笑笑. Xin was still serving as a comptroller general in Nanjing. Yan Huan 嚴煥 (Ziwen) held the same post.

8 You Are the Pinnacle of Smilers

You are the pinnacle of smilers
you don't mind smiling often
and whenever you do it's spring

Even when your singing elicits frowns you smile
if others smile when you're drunk you frown
whether frowning or smiling you elevate our spirits

9 點火櫻桃

點火櫻桃，照一架，荼蘼如雪。
春正好，見龍孫穿破，紫苔蒼壁。
乳燕引雛飛力弱，流鶯喚友嬌聲怯。
問春歸不肯帶愁歸，腸千結。

層樓望，春山疊。
家何在，煙波隔。
把古今遺恨，向他誰說。
蝴蝶不傳千里夢，子規叫斷三更月。
聽聲聲枕上勸人歸，歸難得。

Written to the tune "Whole River Red" in the spring of 1170, most likely in Hangzhou, where Xin was spending time between posts. Xin was still a war émigré living in exile. To the Chinese, the cuckoo's cry sounds like *bu-ru gui-qu* 不如歸去 "better go home."

9 Cherry Blossoms on Fire

Cherry blossoms on fire
lighting a whole trellis
of snow-white raspberry flowers
spring at its best
bamboo shoots breaking through
purple moss-covered slopes
swallows leading chicks to test their wings
zigzagging orioles courting new friends
since spring was leaving I asked if it could take my sorrows too
undo the thousand knots in my heart

I looked out from a tower
at the ridges of newly green hills
toward my home
beyond the mist
about my lifelong regrets
who could I tell
butterflies can't carry a dream that far
beneath the late-night moon a cuckoo called
I listened in bed to its cries urging me to go home
but I can't go home

10 隔戶語春鶯

隔戶語春鶯，纔掛簾兒斂袂行。
漸見淩波羅襪步，盈盈，隨笑隨顰百媚生。

着意聽新聲，盡是司空自教成。
今夜酒腸難道窄，多情，莫放紗籠蠟炬明。

Written to the tune "Man from the South" in the spring of 1170 in Hangzhou. The poems Xin heard that night in the capital's entertainment district were by the poet Sikong Tu 司空圖 (d. 908). Sikong was known for his four-line *jue-ju* 絕句, a Chinese poetic form that was a precursor of what became haiku in Japan. He was especially famous for a series of twenty-four poems about poetry in which he demonstrated its quest for "the effect beyond the tune and the meaning beyond the taste" 韻外之致, 味外之旨. Like Sikong, Xin was also known for his essays on music. Hence his delight in hearing "new sounds."

10 The Orioles Next Door Were Talking About Spring

The orioles next door were talking about spring
I pushed back the curtain gathered my robe and went out
soon I was walking among silk-stockinged throngs
I was overwhelmed
smiling or frowning a hundred charming souls

Hearing new sounds I paid attention
they were all the creation of Sikong
I can't say I didn't drink enough tonight
I was entranced
but please don't shine that lantern

11 直節堂堂

直節堂堂，看夾道冠纓拱立。
漸翠谷羣仙東下，佩環聲急。
誰信天峯飛墮地，傍湖千丈開青壁。
是當年玉斧削方壺，無人識。

山木潤，琅玕濕。
秋露下，瓊珠滴。
向危亭橫跨，玉淵澄碧。
醉舞且搖鸞鳳影，浩哥莫遣魚龍泣。
恨此中風物本吾家，今為客。

Written to the tune "Whole River Red" in the fall of 1170 in Hangzhou, with the note: "At Cold Spring Pavilion" 題冷泉亭. The pavilion was built during the Tang dynasty and still stands, between the front gate of Lingyan Monastery 靈巖寺 and the stream that flows past the Peak That Flew Here 飛來峰 and into nearby West Lake. Teapot Rock was a square rock formation in the lake. "Fish tears" are for show. The character 客, *ke,* meaning "guest," was often used to refer to someone living in exile.

11 So Sheer and Imposing

So sheer and imposing
on both sides officials standing in respect
and immortals from the east descending through the valley
I could hear their jade pendants
but how did this heavenly peak fly here
its towering green wall suddenly appear beside the lake
or someone carve Teapot Rock with a jade axe
and yet no one knows who

The hillsides glistened
with jade bamboo
autumn dew was falling
crystal pearls dripping
a towering pavilion bridged
blue transparent depths
dancing drunk my phoenix shadow swayed
there was no shortage of fish tears in my songs
such sights alas were now my home
and I was a guest

12 東風夜放花千樹

東風夜放花千樹。
更吹落，星如雨。
寶馬雕車香滿路。
風簫聲動，玉壺光轉，一夜魚龍舞。

蛾兒雪柳黄金縷，笑語盈盈暗香去。
眾裏尋他千百度，驀然回首，那人卻在，燈火闌珊處。

Written to the tune "Green Jade Desk," with the note: "New Year's Eve" 元夕, at the beginning of 1171 in Hangzhou, where Xin spent the year serving as secretary of the Court of the National Granaries 司農主簿. Public fireworks displays began in China during the previous century—if not earlier. By Xin Qiji's time, they accompanied the celebration of New Year and the emperor's birthday. The name of China's most popular search engine was taken from this poem: Baidu 百度, which means "a hundred times."

12 In the East Wind Last Night a Thousand Trees Burst Forth

In the east wind last night a thousand trees burst forth
and showered down
a rain of stars
jeweled horses and carriages and incense filled the road
the tremulous sound of a phoenix flute
the transforming glow of a jade vase
all night the lanterns swayed

And she of the moth eyebrows and flower-decked hair
of laughter that beguiles and the subtlest of perfumes
whom I have searched for in crowds a hundred times
as I turned my head
she was there
where the lantern light was faint

13 老來情味減

老來情味減，對別酒，怯流年。
況屈指中秋，十分好月，不照人圓。
無情水都不管，共西風只管送歸船。
秋晚蓴鱸湖上，夜深兒女燈前。

征衫便好去朝天。
玉殿正思賢。
想夜半承明，留教視草，卻遣籌邊。
長安故人問我，道愁腸殢酒只依然。
目斷秋霄落雁，醉來時響空弦。

Written to the tune "Magnolia Flower Lento" in 1172 in Chuzhou 知滁州—across the Yangzi and a day's ride northwest of Nanjing, where Xin was serving as magistrate—with the note: "Seeing off Deputy Magistrate Fan in Chuzhou" 滁州送范倅. Xin's deputy, Fan Ang 范昂, was heading back to the capital. Water shield soup was a specialty of Hangzhou's West Lake. Xin Qiji resigned his post in Chuzhou the following winter due to illness and returned to his in-laws' home in Zhenjiang to recuperate.

13 Our Passions Wane as We Get Older

Our passions wane as we get older
facing goodbye wine
we fear the vanishing years
even more the number of Mid-Autumns
when such lovely moons
won't light our reunions
this unfeeling river's only concern
is to join the west wind in seeing your boat off
to water shield and perch on the lake in fall
your children in lamplight late at night

Dressed for travel you're ready to leave for court
where the palace is looking for worthies
I can imagine your audience at midnight
the request for your suggestions
your strategy for the border
in the capital if friends should ask
say I still keep the pieces of my heart soaked in wine
scanning autumn skies for geese about to land
I imagine hearing bowstrings when I'm drunk

14 流水無情

流水無情，潮到空城頭盡白，離歌一曲怨殘陽。
斷人腸。

東風官柳舞雕牆。
三十六宮花濺淚，春聲何處說興亡。
燕雙雙。

Written to the tune "Wine Spring" in the spring of 1174 in Nanjing, when Xin Qiji returned to serve as assistant to the province's military commissioner. The "broken walls" in the first stanza were in the southwest corner of the city, where the Qinhuai River enters the Yangzi. Although the Song court had restored much of Nanjing to its former glory, the walls along the Yangzi, destroyed at the beginning of the Sui dynasty in 589, remained rubble, and the term "broken walls" was often used to refer to the city. The painted walls in the second stanza were those of the former palace on the north shore of the Qinhuai, which wound its way through the city before reaching the Yangzi.

14 Rivers Have No Feelings

Rivers have no feelings
against the broken walls the waves turn to foam
a farewell song in the merciless fading light
cuts my heart in two

Royal willows dancing in the east wind by painted walls
flowers shedding tears in thirty-six palace chambers
who discusses the state of the world in spring
every pair of swallows

15 獨立蒼茫醉不歸

獨立蒼茫醉不歸。
日暮天寒，歸去來兮。
探梅踏雪幾何時。
今我來思，楊柳依依。

白石岡頭曲岸西，一片閑愁，芳草萋萋。
多情山鳥不須啼。
桃李無言，下自成蹊。

Written to the tune "A Branch of Plum Flowers" in the late spring of 1174 in Nanjing, with the note: "On visiting Jiangshan, for Grand Councillor Ye" 游蔣山，呈葉丞相. Xin Qiji was serving as assistant to Ye Heng 葉衡, the military commissioner for the province of which Nanjing was the capital. Later this year, Ye became grand councillor at the court in Hangzhou. The fact that Xin includes Ye's later title suggests Xin adjusted the note to his poem to reflect Ye's subsequent status. Jiangshan was another name for Nanjing's Zhongshan Mountain 鍾山, which is still famous for its plum trees. White Rock Ridge, also called Rock Ridge 石子岡, was six kilometers southwest of Jiangshan and across the Qinhuai River. It was used as a cemetery by the nobility as early as the Han dynasty. The last couplet refers to the ability of fruit trees to attract visitors, if not for their flowers then for their fruit, whose pits then become new trees, marking the path of such visitors as Xin Qiji and his friend Ye Heng.

15 In the Middle of Nowhere Alone and Still Drinking

In the middle of nowhere alone and still drinking
the sun is setting and it's cold
I should be going home
how often did we search here for plum blossoms in the snow
I'm thinking about that today
surrounded by willows

Across the river on White Rock Ridge
nothing but sorrows
and sweet-smelling plants
I wish the amorous birds wouldn't sing
the plum trees are silent
having made the trail

16 一輪秋影轉金波

一輪秋影轉金波。
飛鏡又重磨。
把酒問姮娥，被白髮，欺人奈何。

乘風好去，長空萬里，直下看山河。
斫去桂婆娑，人道是，清光更多。

Written to the tune “Ceremonial Prelude” in the fall of 1174 in Nanjing, with the note: “A poem for Lu Jiaozan, composed in Jiankang on Mid-Autumn Night” 建康中秋夜為呂叔潛賦. Heng'e, or Chang'e 嫦娥, is the goddess who lives on the moon. Her hair turned white when she became an immortal, and over time it grew to be more than three thousand feet long. While Heng'e's white hair accentuates her beauty, Xin's own reminds him of his lifelong regrets. Even while he tries, if only for a night, to join Heng'e, he hears members of the earthly court far below voicing their worldly concerns. The cassia tree here is the one that grows on the moon and is visible on a clear night. Xin Qiji was still serving as assistant to the military commissioner of the province.

16 To the Autumn Waterwheel Churning Golden Waves

To the autumn waterwheel churning golden waves
the mirror in the sky newly polished again
I raised my cup and asked Heng'e
why does white hair
humiliate us so

As I rode off on the wind
ten thousand miles of sky
mountains and rivers far below me
I heard someone say
If we pruned a few branches
we would have more light

17 楚天千里清秋

楚天千里清秋，水隨天去秋無際。
遙岑遠目，獻愁供恨，玉簪螺髻。
落日樓頭，斷鴻聲裏，江南游子。
把吳鉤看了，欄杆拍邊，無人會，登臨意。

休說鱸魚堪鱠，盡西風季鷹歸未。
求田問舍，怕應羞見，劉郎才氣。
可惜流年，憂愁風雨，樹猶如此。
倩何人喚取，紅巾翠袖，揾英雄淚。

Written to the tune "Water Dragon Song" in 1174 in Nanjing, with the note: "Climbing Shangxin Pavilion" 登建康賞心亭. This pavilion overlooking the Qinhuai River was one of Xin's favorite places and the scene of a number of his poems. Looking toward his home, he couldn't help wondering if he would ever see it again . . . or, in this case, if he would ever use his sword again to help reclaim the country's lost lands. In the second stanza, Zhang Han 張翰, whose sobriquet was Zhiying, "Migratory Hawk," was a southerner who was once asked by Prince Qi to serve as a senior official in his kingdom, whose capital was Luoyang, in the north. As soon as Zhang felt autumn in the air and began to think of his favorite foods in the south, including minced perch, he quit and returned to his home in the Yangzi Delta. Being an exile in the south, Xin feels conflicted about settling down rather than returning to his home in the north and continuing to battle the Jurchens. He is also reminded of Liu Bei's ceaseless energy in his own quest, which is recorded in the early historical novel *Romance of the Three Kingdoms.* Silk scarves and sleeves were common attire for female entertainers.

17 A Southern Sky a Thousand Miles of Autumn Air

A southern sky a thousand miles of autumn air
the river disappearing into the boundless fall horizon
distant peaks far-off eyes
sadness and regret
jade hairpins and snail hairdos
the sun setting beyond the pavilion
the sudden sound of geese
an exile south of the Yangzi
inspecting his bronze blade
rubbing the railing
no one understands
what climbing here means

Don't tell me about minced perch
or say hawks don't migrate in fall
if I looked for some land to farm
I would likely be embarrassed
by the spirit of Liu Bei
I bemoan the passing years
saddened by the wind and rain
and these trees still here
who can I call
with a silk scarf or sleeve
to wipe a hero's tears

18 青山欲共高人語

青山欲共高人語，聯翩萬馬來無數。
烟雨卻低回，望來終不來。

人言頭山髮，總向愁中白。
拍手笑沙鷗，一身都是愁。

Written to the tune "Bodhisattva Barbarian" in the spring of 1175, with the note: "Poem for Grand Councillor Ye at Jinling's Shangxin Pavilion" 金陵賞心亭為葉丞相賦. Ye Heng left Nanjing at the end of 1174 to become grand councillor at court in Lin'an and arranged for Xin Qiji to have an audience with Emperor Xiaozong later that year. Xin's attempt to change the emperor's policy of appeasement failed once again. Jinling was another name for Nanjing.

18 The Mountains Wish to Speak with the Master

The mountains wish to speak with the Master
more than ten thousand teams of prancing horses
hesitate in the mist and rain
despite their hopes he doesn't come

People say the hair on our heads
turns white due to sorrow
I clap and laugh at the gulls
embodiments of sadness

19 鬱孤臺下清江水

鬱孤臺下清江水，中間多少行人淚。
西北望長安，可憐無數山。

青山遮不住，畢竟東流去。
江晚正愁余，山深聞鷓鴣。

Written to the tune "Bodhisattva Barbarian" in 1176, with the note: "Written on a wall at Zaokou in Jiangxi" 書江西造口壁. This pavilion was located on a hill in Ganzhou 贛州 and overlooked the Gan River 贛江, a major tributary of the Yangzi. Zaokou was about twenty kilometers downriver from Ganzhou. The previous year, Xin Qiji was made judicial commissioner of Jiangxi province and was also put in charge of the local army during a rebellion led by tea merchants unwilling to pay the government tax on tea. After putting down the rebellion, Xin was heading back to his headquarters in Nanchang 南昌 (Yucheng) when he wrote this. When the Jurchens sacked the Song capital of Kaifeng in 1126, over a million Chinese fled south, pursued by Jurchen forces even beyond the Yangzi. Many of those who survived settled in towns along the Gan River, where this poem was written. Once the Gan's waters join the Yangzi, they flow east until they reach the sea. The partridge, or Chinese francolin, is common in the Yangzi watershed but not in northern China. Hearing its cry was just another reminder of how far Xin was from home.

19 The Clear Waters Below Yugu Pavilion

The clear waters below Yugu Pavilion
carry the tears of so many refugees
looking north toward our old capital
I can't count all the mountains

The mountains don't block the waters
the waters eventually flow east
the river at dusk breaks my heart
somewhere on the mountain a partridge is calling

20 野棠花落

野棠花落，又匆匆過了，清明時節。
剗地東風欺客夢，一夜雲屏寒怯。
曲岸持觴，垂楊繫馬，此地曾經別。
樓空人去，舊遊飛燕能說。

聞道綺陌東頭，行人長見，簾底纖纖月。
舊恨春江流不斷，新恨雲山千疊。
料得明朝，尊前重見，鏡裏花難折。
也應驚問，近來多少華髮。

Written to the tune "Recalling a Pretty Girl" in late spring of 1178, with the note: "Written on a wall in Dongliu Village" 書東流村壁. Xin Qiji stopped here on his way back to Nanjing from Nanchang, where he was serving as military and judicial commissioner of Jiangxi province. This village was near the Yangzi port of Chizhou 池州, two hundred kilometers upriver from Nanjing, where Li Bai had immortalized the beauty of the local women. The practice of foot-binding, which began just before the start of the Song dynasty, was embraced by its rulers and nobility and remained popular in China for a thousand years, through the beginning of the twentieth century.

20 Wild Pear Blossoms Are Falling

Wild pear blossoms are falling
once more I have survived
Purification Day
the heartless spring wind and another deceptive dream
shivering all night behind a mica screen
after tying our horses to the willows
we raised our cups on that winding bank
where we last parted
she's not there anymore
though about that time the swallows still talk

At the east end of the silk-lined street
I hear passersby still see her
behind the curtain her crescent-moon feet
old regrets are like rivers that flood every spring
new ones like a thousand more cloud-shrouded ridges
I wonder if tomorrow
I met her over wine again
how hard it would be to pick a flower in a mirror
and would she likely be startled
by all this white hair

21 撲面往塵去路遙

撲面往塵去路遙，香篝漸覺水沉銷。
山無重數周遭碧，花不知名分外嬌。

人歷歷，馬蕭蕭，旌旗又過小紅橋。
愁邊剩有相思句，搖斷吟鞭碧玉梢。

Written to the tune "Partridge Sky" in 1178 in Hangzhou, with the note: "On the Road to Dongyang" 東陽道中. Xin Qiji was serving as vice minister of the court of judicial review and was traveling on an assignment to Dongyang—a hundred kilometers south of the capital. At least as far back as Qu Yuan 屈原 (d. 278 BCE), men wore sachets of flowers whose fragrances were said to represent the wearer's virtues in addition to having different effects on the wearer.

21 Face Covered with Dust and Still Far to Go

Face covered with dust and still far to go
his sachet's perfume beginning to fade
no end to mountains all directions green
flowers he's never seen exceptionally lovely

I see him clearly
his panting horse
his banner crossing that little red bridge again
besides being anxious he's in love
I hear the whack of his jade-crested whip

22 千丈懸崖削翠

千丈懸崖削翠，一川落日鎔金。
白鷗來往本無心，選甚風波一任。

別浦魚肥堪膾，前村酒美重斟。
千年往事已沉沉，閑管興亡則甚。

Written to the tune "West River Moon" in 1178, with the note: "Traveling on the Yangzi at Caishi, I wrote this 'Fisherman-style' lyric for fun" 江行采石岸，戲作漁父詞. Xin Qiji stopped at Caishi while traveling up the Yangzi to serve as deputy fiscal commissioner of Hubei province. Caishi was located one hundred kilometers south of Nanjing and was where Jurchen naval forces tried to mount an invasion of the Southern Song in 1161 from the Yangzi's north shore. Through the use of incendiary bombs containing gunpowder, and maneuverable, treadmill-operated paddle-wheel ships, the Southern Song destroyed the Jurchen fleet. Xin Qiji's poem emulates Qu Yuan's "The Fisherman," in which a fisherman makes fun of Qu Yuan's own righteous distress. Minced perch was a favorite dish in the lower reaches of the Yangzi. Shortly after writing this, Xin received news that his assignment was changed from Hubei to Hunan province, where another rebellion had broken out.

22 A Thousand-Foot Cliff of Sheer Green

A thousand-foot cliff of sheer green
the river at sunset molten gold
seagulls flying past unimpressed
riding the ever-changing wind and waves

Fish from the delta perfect for mincing
wine in the village good enough to pour
events of a thousand years gone without a trace
who cares what once happened here

23 山前燈火欲黃昏

山前燈火欲黃昏，山頭來去雲。
鷓鴣聲裏數家村，瀟湘逢故人。

揮羽扇，整綸巾，少年鞍馬塵。
如今憔悴賦招魂，儒冠多誤身。

Written to the tune "Master Ruan Goes Home" in the summer of 1179, with the note: "On the way to Leiyang, written for Judge Zhang Chufu" 耒陽道中為張處父推官賦. Fans and caps such as Xin describes were used by officials at court during earlier dynasties. Xin Qiji was now serving as deputy fiscal commissioner for Hunan and wrote this on his way to deal with an insurrection caused by excessive taxation. He was traveling up the Xiang River 湘江, then overland to the east toward Leiyang, which was two hundred kilometers south of Changsha 常沙. In the second stanza, Xin thinks back to fifteen years earlier when he and Zhang Chufu met at court during an audience with the emperor. The poem "Calling the Departed" was written by Song Yu 宋玉 (d. 222 BCE), successor of the shaman-poet Qu Yuan. Known for his righteousness like Qu Yuan, Song tries to summon Qu Yuan's spirit. Xin Qiji was an active participant in the neo-Confucian renaissance of his time.

23 Lights on the Mountain Just Before Dusk

Lights on the mountain just before dusk
clouds drifting past the summit
a hillside village a partridge's call
meeting an old friend on the Xiang

Holding feather fans
wearing silk caps
we raised the dust when we were young
worn-out now we sing "Calling the Departed"
Confucians mostly make a mess of their lives

24 稼軒日向兒童說

稼軒日向兒童說，帶湖買得新風月。
頭白早歸來，種花花已開。

功名渾是錯，更莫思量着。
見說小樓東，好山千萬里重。

Written to the tune "Bodhisattva Barbarian" in 1181 in Shangrao upon the completion of his new home. "Little Pavilion" refers to Jishan Pavilion 集山樓. Jiaxuan 稼軒 (Farmhouse) was the pen name Xin chose for himself when he retired to Ribbon Lake. The lake was the widening of a river caused by an earthen dam just outside the north gate of Shangrao. His residence was on the east shore of the lake, and Little Pavilion, which was built earlier by someone else, was at the summit of the ridge behind his house. Xin Qiji was technically still serving as military commissioner of Jiangxi and magistrate of Longxing 隆興 (an old name for Nanchang, the capital of Jiangxi). Sensing his enemies at court were gaining the upper hand, he decided to prepare for his "retirement" in advance. He purchased this land and began work on his Ribbon Lake residence in 1178. It was not a simple home and took several years to complete. For details, see 辛弃疾信州词与信州生活 (Xin Qiji's Lyric Poems and Life in the Shangrao Area). The new residence was finished just in time. At the end of this year, Xin's next appointment as judicial commissioner of Zhejiang was canceled, and he was relieved of all duties as the result of one of his critics' charges that he had wasted government money and had been insensitive to the suffering of the people.

24 Jiaxuan Told His Children One Day

Jiaxuan told his children one day
I bought a scenic place on Ribbon Lake
since my hair was turning white it was time to retire
the flowers I planted are already blooming

Chasing success and fame were mistakes
they no longer occupy my thoughts
east of Little Pavilion I have heard
the mountains stretch for ten thousand miles

25 帶湖我甚愛

帶湖我甚愛，千丈翠奩開。
先生杖屨無事，一日走千回。
凡我同盟鷗鷺，今日既盟之後，來往莫相猜。
白鶴在何處，嘗試與偕來。

破青萍，排翠藻，立蒼苔。
窺魚笑汝癡計，不解舉吾杯。
廢沼荒丘疇昔，明月清風此夜，人世幾歡哀。
東岸綠陰少，楊柳更須栽。

Written to the tune "Water Music Song" in the spring of 1182 at Daihu Lake, with the note: "Pact with the seagulls" 盟鷗. Women in China and elsewhere in East Asia used wooden makeup boxes, the tops of which slid open to form standing mirrors. Among the tales of Liezi 列子, a Daoist raconteur of the fourth century BCE, "Every day a fisherman went walking along the beach. As he did, flocks of seagulls accompanied him. One day his father asked him to catch one, so he could keep one as a pet. After that, whenever the fisherman went walking on the beach, the seagulls kept their distance" (*Liezi* 2.11). Xin has made his own agreement with the gulls: "to do no harm."

25 How I Love Ribbon Lake

How I love Ribbon Lake
the green mile-long open makeup box
with my cane and sandals and nothing to do
I walk back and forth a thousand times a day
as for the gulls with whom I'm now in league
after our agreement today
they won't need to worry
where is that crane
he can join us too

Breaking apart the duckweed
pushing aside the algae
he stands on the moss
I smile at his silly plans involving fish
and his inability to join me for a drink
where there once was a watery wasteland
there's a full moon and cool breeze tonight
how many people in the world are happy
the east shore could use more shade
I need to plant more willows

26 少日春懷似酒濃

少日春懷似酒濃，插花走馬醉千鍾。
老去逢春如病酒，唯有，茶甌香篆小簾櫳。

卷盡殘花風未定，休恨，花開元自要春風。
試問春歸誰得見，飛燕，來時相遇夕陽中。

Written to the tune "Calming the Wind and Waves" in 1182 at his Ribbon Lake residence, with the note: "Late spring inspiration" 暮春漫興.

26 I Loved Spring as Much as Wine When I Was Young

I loved spring as much as wine when I was young
I picked flowers on horseback and drank without restraint
older now I view spring like a hangover
give me
tea and incense and smaller window screens

After blowing away the last petals the wind doesn't stop
or the longing
flowers open so they can feel the warmer air
if you wonder who sees where spring goes
it's the swallows
they meet it at sunset the day they arrive

27 小小年華才月半

小小年華才月半。
羅幕春風，幸自無人見。
剛道羞郎低粉面，旁人瞥見回嬌盼。

昨夜西池陪女伴。
柳困花慵，見說歸來晚。
勸客持觴渾未慣，未歌先覺花枝顫。

Written to the tune "A Butterfly's Favorite Flower" in 1182 in Shangrao about an evening spent in nearby Yanshan's West Lake, with the note: "Presented to Yang Qingweng's female attendant at a party" 席上贈楊濟翁侍兒. Yang Qingweng (aka Yang Jiweng) and Xin Qiji exchanged a number of poems. Yang also stayed with Xin at his Daihu residence. This and the next poem were likely written on the same occasion.

27 So Young in Years Just Fifteen

So young in years just fifteen
regarding spring breezes behind silk curtains
she has naturally yet to know
as a shy youth spoke she covered her face
onlookers noticed how sweetly she looked back

At West Lake last night she joined some older women
drooping willows and faded flowers
I heard she returned home late
not used to urging guests to drink
like a branch of blossoms she trembled before she sang

28 淚眼送君傾似雨

淚眼送君傾似雨。
不折垂楊，只倩愁隨去。
有底風光留不住，煙波萬頃春江艫。

老馬臨流癡不渡。
應惜障泥，忘了尋春路。
身在稼軒安穩處，書來不用多行數。

Written to the tune "A Butterfly's Favorite Flower" in 1182 at his home outside Shangrao, with the note: "Continuing Yang Jiweng's rhyme and presented to Magistrate Fan Nanbo on his way back to Jingkou" 繼楊濟翁韻餞范南伯知縣歸京口. Fan Nanbo was Xin Qiji's wife's brother. It was common for someone to give a friend leaving on a journey a willow catkin, as the names for "willow" and "stay" were homophones. The first stanza recounts seeing Fan off at the nearby port of Yanshan. Although both Shangrao and Yanshan were on the Xinjiang River 信江, passenger boats heading for the Yangzi via Poyang Lake 鄱陽湖 left from Yanshan, where the water was much deeper due to the conflux with the Yanhe River 鉛河 just east of town. Horses were outfitted with leather on either flank to keep mud off the rider. This story was cited in the *Shishuo Xinyu* 世說新語 as an example of a horse that had its own priorities over those of the rider, who was looking, in this case, for the first signs of spring. In the penultimate line, Xin refers to his pen name: Jiaxuan (Farmhouse).

28 When We Said Goodbye Our Tears Fell Like Rain

When we said goodbye our tears fell like rain
instead of breaking off a willow catkin
I sent you off with sorrow
I couldn't stop anything that day
not the endless waves of spring not your boat on the river

The reason the old horse was "too stupid" to cross the stream
was to keep its mudguards clean
it didn't care about searching for spring
here at my peaceful farmhouse
I don't need to say much when I write

29 一天霜月明

一天霜月明，幾處砧聲起。
客夢已難成，秋色無邊際。

旦夕是重陽，菊有黃花蕊。
只怕又登高，未飲心先醉。

Written to the tune "Fresh Hawthorn Berries" in 1183, with the note: "Matching the rhyme of Xia Zhongyu" 和夏中玉. This was one of two poems Xin wrote matching the rhyme of this friend about whom we know nothing else. Although Xin had retired to Daihu Lake, he wrote this while on a brief mission to Yangzhou, across the Yangzi from Zhenjiang. This was the time of year when women beat their clothing with mallets to flatten the fibers in order to keep the wind from penetrating the fabric. On Double Ninth men put chrysanthemum stamens—the heart of the flower—in their wine and sometimes petals too. This festival is a conjunction of symbols for *yang* 陽, or male, energy. The Chinese characters for *chrysanthemum, old, wine,* and *nine* were all pronounced the same during the Song.

29 A Frosty Sky a Brilliant Moon

A frosty sky a brilliant moon
the occasional sound of a mallet
it's hard for an exile to sleep
with signs of fall filling the horizon

Tomorrow is Double Ninth
chrysanthemum petal time
I worry if I climb somewhere high again
I'll feel drunk without drinking

30 陌上柔桑破嫩芽

陌上柔桑破嫩芽，東鄰蠶種已生些。
平岡細草鳴黃犢，斜日寒林點暮鴉。

山遠近，路橫斜，青旗沽酒有人家。
城中桃李愁風雨，春在溪頭薺菜花。

Written to the tune "Partridge Sky" between 1184 and 1186 at his Daihu Lake residence, with the note: "Written for someone" 代人賦.

30 Mulberries Along the Path Unfurling Their Leaves

Mulberries along the path unfurling their leaves
the neighbor's silkworms already stirring
new grass on the hill the sound of bawling calves
leafless woods at sunset the sight of returning crows

On mountains far or near
roads steep or level
wherever there's a wine flag there're people
flowering trees in town dread the wind and rain
in spring along the streams there's shepherd's purse in bloom

31 著意尋春懶便回

着意尋春懶便回，何如信步兩三杯。
山纔好處行還倦，詩未成時雨早催。

攜竹杖，更芒鞋，朱朱粉粉野蒿開。
誰家寒食歸寧女，笑語柔桑陌上來。

Written to the tune "Partridge Sky" in 1186, with the note: "Written after coming back from Ehu and feeling ill" 鵝湖歸，病起作. This is one of three poems to which Xin Qiji added the same note. Ehu, or Goose Lake, was twenty kilometers southwest of Shangrao and the location of the neo-Confucian academy founded by his friend Zhu Xi. Coming home from their in-laws' to their own parents' houses this time of year, these girls will soon be busy feeding the new mulberry leaves to silkworms and weaving silk to help their parents pay taxes. Cold Food Day occurs in early April, 105 days after the winter solstice.

31 I Tried to Find Spring and Came Back Exhausted

I tried to find spring and came back exhausted
I should have let my feet lead me to some wine
mountains are fine but not when you're tired
before this poem was done it started to rain

I put on rope sandals and grabbed my cane
the rosy-red mugwort was blooming
whose daughters were those coming home on Cold Food Day
laughing as they walked past the new mulberry leaves

32 一榻清風殿影涼

一榻清風殿影涼，涓涓流水響回廊。
千章雲木鉤輈叫，十里溪風䆉稏香。

衝急雨，趁斜陽，山園細路轉微茫。
倦途卻被行人笑，只有林泉有底忙。

Written to the tune "Partridge Sky" in the summer of 1186, with the note: "Along the road to Ehu Temple" 鵝湖寺道中. Ehu Temple, southwest of Shangrao, was just beyond Ehu Academy 鵝湖書院, established by Xin's friend Zhu Xi and one of China's most famous Confucian centers, one where the intricacies of neo-Confucian thought were debated—occasionally by Xin Qiji as well.

32 A Cot Cooled by a Breeze in the Shade of a Shrine

A cot cooled by a breeze in the shade of a shrine
on a covered walkway beside babbling water
partridges calling from a cloud-wrapped forest
ripening rice perfuming a stream for ten miles

Gusting rain
fading light
the trail through terraced fields disappearing into the weeds
my slow progress arousing the laughter of others
it's the woods and springs that distract me

33 補陀大士虛空

補陀大士虛空，翠巖誰記飛來處。
蜂房萬點，似穿如礙，玲瓏窗戶。
石髓千年，已垂未落，嶙峋冰柱。
有怒濤聲遠，落花香在，人疑是，桃源路。

又說春雷鼻息，是臥龍彎環如許。
不然應是，洞庭張樂，湘靈來去。
我意長松，倒生陰壑，細吟風雨。
竟茫茫未曉，只應白髮，是開山祖。

Written to the tune "Water Music Song" around 1186, with the note: "Written about Yuyan Cliff. There is a painting of Guanyin Bodhisattva on the cliff and a cascade that sounds like the wind and rain" 題雨巖. 巖類今所畫觀音補陀. 巖中有泉飛出, 如風雨聲. The cliff and its limestone caverns were an hour's hike west of Boshan Temple 博山寺. Tao Yuanming once authored a tale he titled "Peach Blossom Spring," in which a fisherman traced peach petals in a stream to their source, passing through an opening in the rocks to a land lost in time. The wives of Emperor Shun 舜帝 (d. 2184 BCE) became the spirits of Dongting Lake 洞庭湖 when, after hearing their husband had died, they drowned themselves in its waters. The poet Qu Yuan also drowned himself in a tributary of the same lake, the main source of which is the Xiang River.

33 Great Bodhisattva of Emptiness

Great Bodhisattva of Emptiness
where did your jade cliff come from
your ten thousand beehives
half open half closed
like finely carved doors or windows
your ancient stalactites
hanging suspended
fluted pillars of ice
the distant sound of crashing waves
the scent of fallen flowers
people wonder
if this isn't the way to Peach Blossom Spring

Some say it's the thunderous snoring
of a sleeping coiled dragon
or maybe
Dongting Lake music
the spirits of the Xiang
I think it's a big pine tree
down in the ravine
its faint song of the wind and rain
in the end who knows
why not the old man
who came here first

34 春入平原薺菜花

春入平原薺菜花，新耕雨後落群鴉。
多情白髮春無奈，晚日青簾酒易賒。

閒意態，細生涯，牛欄西畔有桑麻。
青裙縞袂誰家女，去趁蠶生看外家。

Written to the tune "Partridge Sky" in the spring of 1187, with the note: "Written on a wineshop wall while drunk during a visit to Ehu" 遊鵝湖醉書酒家壁. Shepherd's purse is a low-growing plant found along ditches and abandoned land and a welcome addition to the meal of anyone short on rations. A poem about farm life. The hemp was for supplying the family with clothing, the mulberries for taxes, which were paid in lengths of silk. A blue dye was produced from the indigo plant.

34 Shepherd's Purse Flowering on the Plain in Spring

Shepherd's purse flowering on the plain in spring
crows landing on a plowed field after a rain
hair white from worry I'm helpless in spring
blue flags at sunset not hard to buy wine

Easygoing manners
horizonless lives
west of the stables mulberry and hemp
who was that wearing the blue skirt and white sleeves
hurrying to her parents to check on the silkworms

35 未到山前騎馬回

未到山前騎馬回，風吹雨打已無梅。
共誰消遣兩三杯。

一似舊時春意思，百無是處老形骸。
也曾頭上戴花來。

Written to the tune "Washing Silk in the River" in the spring of 1187, with the note: "Written on impulse" 漫與作.

35 Before Reaching the Mountain I Turned My Horse Around

Before reaching the mountain I turned my horse around
heavy wind and rain and no plum blossoms
or anyone to share a few cups of wine

Same as always thinking of spring
no part of my body doesn't feel old
despite once wearing flowers in my hair

36 烟蕪露麥荒池柳

烟蕪露麥荒池柳，洗雨烘晴。
洗雨烘晴，一様春風幾様青。

提壺脫袴推歸去，萬恨千情。
萬恨千情，各自無聊各自鳴。

To the tune "Ugly Servant" in 1187, with the note: "Written on a wall on the Boshan Road" 書博山道中壁. Once he settled just outside Shangrao, Xin Qiji was a frequent visitor at Boshan Mountain and its Buddhist monastery—twenty kilometers from his home to the east. "Pot Holder" and "Ragged Pants" are birds, namely, the pelican (*ti-hu* 鵜鶘) and the cuckoo (*bu-gu* 布穀), whose names in Chinese are made fun of here through the use of homophones.

36 On the Weeds on the Wheat on the Willows by the Pond

On the weeds on the wheat on the willows by the pond
it drizzles then it bakes
it drizzles then it bakes
the same spring breeze different shades of green

Pot Holder and Ragged Pants tell spring to go away
ten thousand regrets a thousand kinds of love
ten thousand regrets a thousand kinds of love
each and every heartbreak each and every song

37 隱隱輕靁

隱隱輕靁，雨聲不受春回護。
落梅如許，吹盡墻邊去。

春水無情，礙斷溪南路。
憑誰訴，寄聲傳語，沒人知處。

Written to the tune "Painted Red Lips" in 1187, with the note: "While staying at Boshan Temple, I heard Mister Guangfeng went home feeling ill and the spring flood destroyed the bridge" 留博山寺, 聞光風主人微恙而歸, 時春漲斷橋. The identity of Guangfeng is unknown. In addition to its monastery, Boshan was home to solitary practitioners of various kinds.

37 The Faint Peal of Thunder

The faint peal of thunder
spring couldn't hold back the rain
so many plum blossoms
blown against the wall

The flood was heartless
cutting off the road south
who can I tell
I want to send a letter
but no one knows your address

38 不向長安路上行

不向長安路上行。
卻教山寺厭逢迎。
味無味處求吾樂，材不材間過此生。

寧作我，豈其卿。
人間走遍卻歸耕。
一松一竹真朋友，山鳥山花好弟兄。

To the tune "Partridge Sky" in 1187, with the note: "Written at Boshan Temple" 博山寺作. The ancient capital of Chang'an is a stand-in here for the Southern Song capital of Hangzhou, the location of the court—and the best jobs.

38 I Didn't Take the Road to Chang'an

I didn't take the road to Chang'an
I've worn out my welcome at mountain temples
pursuing the pleasure of tasting the tasteless
passing my time training to be untrained

I preferred to be me
not some official
having traveled the realm I retired to farm
pine trees and bamboo are my truest friends
wildflowers and birds my dearest brothers

39 少年不識愁滋味

少年不識愁滋味，愛上層樓。
愛上層樓，為賦新詞強說愁。

而今識盡愁滋味，欲說還休。
欲說還休，卻道天涼好個秋。

To the tune "Ugly Servant" around 1187, with the note: "Written on a wall on the Boshan Road" 書博山道中壁.

39 I Didn't Know the Taste of Sadness When I Was Young

I didn't know the taste of sadness when I was young
I loved to climb towers
I loved to climb towers
and in my poems I forced myself to speak of sadness

Knowing the taste of sadness now too well
I start to speak of it then stop
I start to speak of it then stop
and say instead *What a chilly autumn day*

40 身世酒杯中

身世酒杯中，萬事皆空。
古來三五個英雄。
雨打風吹何處是，漢殿秦宮。

夢入少年叢，歌舞匆匆。
老僧夜半誤鳴鐘。
驚起西窗眠不得，捲地西風。

Written to the tune "Sifting Sand" (as in panning for gold) in the fall of 1187 at Daihu Lake, with the note: "Hearing the bell at a mountain temple at midnight" 山寺夜半聞鐘. Buddhist monks usually rang their bells just before they retired for the night. One noteworthy exception was at Hanshan Temple 寒山寺 in Suzhou, where the monks rang "the bell of impermanence," as they called it, at midnight. The west wind of autumn also reminded people about impermanence. The heroes Xin often mentions include Cao Cao, Liu Bei, and Sun Zhongmou 孫仲謀, who fought one another in an effort to reestablish the dominion of the Han dynasty, which replaced the Qin.

40 I've Spent My Life in a Wine Cup

I've spent my life in a wine cup
whatever I've done has been in vain
in the past a few heroes
faced the wind and rain
but where is Qin Palace or Han Hall

I was dreaming about my younger days
the singing and dancing were a blur
at midnight an old monk rang his bell by mistake
unable to go back to sleep I opened the west window
the autumn wind was relentless

41 暗香橫路雪垂垂

暗香橫路雪垂垂，晚風吹，曉風吹。
花意爭春，先出歲寒枝。
畢竟一年春事了，緣太早，卻成遲。

未應全是雪霜姿，欲開時，未開時。
粉面朱唇，一半點胭脂。
醉裏謗花花莫恨，渾冷澹，有誰知。

Written to the tune "River God" at the end of 1187 just before New Year, with the note: "A poem about plum blossoms sent to Yu Shulang" 賦梅寄余叔良. Commentators think the recipient was a recluse who wrote poems and also lived in the Shangrao area.

41 From a Net of Suspended Snow a Hidden Fragrance

From a net of suspended snow a hidden fragrance
blown by the wind at dusk
blown by the wind at dawn
your blossoms were hoping to beat spring
appearing on bare branches before New Year
as for being part of spring
you're too early
also too late

You're not at all like the snow
you want to bloom
but before you do
to your powdered face and red lips
you add a touch of rouge
being drunk I malign you not that you care
you're so utterly aloof
nobody knows you

42 溪邊照影行

溪邊照影行，天在清溪底。
天上有行雲，人在行雲裏。

高歌誰和余，空谷清音起。
非鬼亦非仙，一曲桃花水。

Written to the tune "Fresh Hawthorn Berries" around 1187 on Boshan, with the note: "Hiking alone near Yuyan Cliff" 獨游雨巖. This cliff was an hour's hike west of Boshan Monastery. The reference in the last line is to Tao Yuanming's "Peach Blossom Spring" and to a world gratefully cut off from ours—the Chinese version of Shangri-la.

42 Walking Along a Stream I See My Reflection

Walking along a stream I see my reflection
at the bottom of the stream is the sky
in the sky clouds are drifting
in the clouds I am walking

Who is that singing along with me
that pure voice from a deserted valley
not a ghost or immortal
singing about peach petals in a stream

43 一川松竹任橫斜

一川松竹任橫斜，有人家，被雲遮。
雪後疏梅，時見兩三花。
比着桃源溪上路，風景好，不爭多。

旗亭有酒徑須賒，晚寒些，怎禁他。
醉裏匆匆，歸騎自隨車。
白髮蒼顏吾老矣，只此地，是生涯。

Written to the tune "River God" around 1187, with the note: "On the Boshan Road, I wrote this on Mister Wang's wall" 博山道中書王氏壁. Mister Wang operated a winery (for rice wine) on the mountain. The first line describes what must have been the detritus of a logging operation—most likely the result of the massive shipbuilding undertaken by the Southern Song, not only for protection from the Jurchens but also for expanding trade with Southeast Asian kingdoms and beyond. The reference to Yuanming's story about a hidden land discovered by tracing peach petals in a stream also appears in poems 5, 33, and 42.

43 Pines and Bamboo Scattered Here and There

Pines and bamboo scattered here and there
and people
hidden in the clouds
on the plum trees after a snowfall
I saw a few blossoms
compared to the road to Peach Blossom Spring
the scenery
about the same

There was a store and I needed some wine
the evening chill
was hard to bear
drunk and in a blur
on horseback I followed a cart home
white-haired weathered face and feeling old
this is the place
where I live

44 柳邊飛鞚

柳邊飛鞚，露濕征衣重。
宿鷺窺沙孤影動，應有漁蝦入夢。

一川淡月疏星，浣紗人影娉婷。
笑背行人歸去，門前稚子啼聲。

Written to the tune "Peace and Purity" around 1187, with the note: "Sights on the Boshan Road" 博山道中即事.

44 Bridles Fly past the Willows

Bridles fly past the willows
dew soaks the riders' clothes
the shadow of a roosting egret staring at the sand moves
fish and shrimp no doubt in its dream

A river of pale moonlight and scattered stars
the reflection of a woman washing clothes
smiling at a passerby she turns and disappears
the sound of a child crying inside the door

45 青山招不來

青山招不來，偃蹇誰憐汝。
歲晚太寒生，喚我溪邊住。

山頭明月來，本在天高處。
夜夜入青溪，聽讀離騷去。

Written to the tune "Fresh Hawthorn Berries" around 1187, with the note: "Hiking at West Cliff alone" 獨游西岩. This cliff was on Boshan. Qu Yuan's "Li Sao" 離騷 ("Beset by Sorrow") was a frequent source of inspiration for Xin Qiji. Here are a few examples of its ninety-three quatrains: "Blessed with an abundance of inner beauty / to which I added arts and skills / I wore angelica and lovage / sewed autumn orchids into my sash" (3); "I sip magnolia dew in the morning / dine on chrysanthemum petals at night / as long as my waist reflects my inner beauty / what harm is a sallow complexion" (17); "Alas in this land where none understands me / why should I care for its ancient capital / since no one is able to govern with beauty / I shall go where Peng and Xian dwell" (93). Peng 彭 and Xian 憲 were two shamans associated with the origin of medicine and divination, respectively.

45 Mountains Aren't Servants

Mountains aren't servants
who doesn't love their unbending nature
when the year-end turns cold
they tell me to stand beside a stream

Once the moon rises above the ridge
and climbs high enough in the sky
night after night it enters the dark water
and listens to me read "Beset by Sorrow"

46 連雲松竹

連雲松竹，萬事從今足。
拄杖東家分社肉，白酒床頭初熟。

西風梨棗山園，兒童偷把長竿。
莫遣旁人驚去，老夫靜處閒看。

Written to the tune "Peace and Purity" in the 1180s, with the note: "Inspecting a mountain orchard and reporting what I saw" 檢校山園，書所見. The dates in the orchard are Chinese red dates, *Ziziphus jujuba.*

46 The Pines and Bamboo Merged with the Clouds

The pines and bamboo merged with the clouds
everything that moment was perfect
the landlord was dividing the meat with his cane
the rice mash had just been pressed

The dates in the orchard felt the fall air
a child was stealing them with a pole
not wanting onlookers to scare him away
the old man watched in silence

47 梨花着雨晚來晴

梨花着雨晚來晴。
月朧明，淚縱横。
繡閣香濃，深鎖鳳簫聲。
未必人知春意思，還獨自，遶花行。

酒兵昨夜壓愁城。
太狂生，轉關情。
寫盡胸中，塊磊未全平。
卻與平章珠玉價，看醉裏，錦囊傾。

Written to the tune "River God" in the 1180s at his home in Shangrao, with the note: "Matching someone else's rhyme" 和人韻.

47 It Rained on the Pear Blossoms Then at Dusk It Cleared

It rained on the pear blossoms then at dusk it cleared
the moon was obscured
streaked with tears
the heavy perfume of the women's quarters
the muffled sound of a flute in the wind
no one else knew what spring was thinking
no one except me
circling the blossoms

Last night this drunk soldier toppled walls of sorrow
acted crazy
about love it turned out
writing down what was in my heart
I didn't quite level all the ramparts
assessing the value of my jewels
and doing it drunk
I emptied my purse

48 鐘鼎山林都是夢

鐘鼎山林都是夢，人間寵辱休驚。
只消閑處過平生。
酒杯秋吸露，詩句夜裁冰。

記取小窗風雨夜，對牀燈火多情。
問誰千里伴君行。
曉山眉樣翠，秋水鏡般明。

Written to the tune "Immortal by the River" in the 1180s in Shangrao, with the note: "Using the previous rhyme again and seeing off my younger cousin Youzhi, who was returning to Fuliang" 再用前韻送祐之弟歸浮梁. Fuliang was a hundred kilometers northwest of Shangrao.

48 Whether at Court or in the Woods Life Is a Dream

Whether at court or in the woods life is a dream
don't be startled when you're praised or blamed
pass your life someplace quiet instead
with a wine cup in autumn filled with dew
a few lines at night carved in ice

Do you remember that rainy night below my little window
happy in our beds facing the lantern light
I asked who was joining you on your thousand-mile journey
at dawn over mountains like eyebrows painted green
in autumn down rivers clearer than a mirror

49 遶床饑鼠

遶床饑鼠，蝙蝠翻燈舞。
屋上松風吹急雨，破紙窗間自語。

平生塞北江南，歸來華髮蒼顏。
布被秋宵夢覺，眼前萬里江山。

Written to the tune "Peace and Purity" in the 1180s, with the note: "Spending the night alone at Mister Wang's hermitage on Boshan" 獨宿博山王氏菴.

49 Hungry Mice Circle My Bed

Hungry mice circle my bed
bats pirouette above the lamp
a heavy forest rain beats against the roof
shredded paper panes chatter in the wind

Having spent my life on both sides of the Yangzi
I've retired dark skinned and gray haired
on a fall night beneath a blanket I woke from a dream
a thousand miles of mountains and rivers before my eyes

50 夜深殘月過山房

夜深殘月過山房，睡覺北窗涼。
起遶中庭獨步，一天星斗文章。

朝來客話，山林鍾鼎，那處難忘。
君向沙頭細問，白鷗知我行藏。

Written to the tune "Goings-On at Court" in the 1180s on Boshan. This was one of two poems he wrote on this occasion. The roof was that of the hermitage Xin Qiji constructed near Yuyan Cliff. The shore Xin is referring to is that of the Fengxi River, which flowed past the southern foot of the mountain. Xin Qiji had a special relationship with seagulls, namely, to do no harm. See also poems 25 and 53.

50 After the Gibbous Moon Crossed the Roof Last Night

After the gibbous moon crossed the roof last night
cold air from the north window woke me
I got up and walked around the courtyard alone
nothing but patterns of stars in the sky

The next morning somebody asked
Life in the woods or at court
which is harder to forget
go down to the shore and ask around
the seagulls know which I prefer

51 明月別枝驚鵲

明月別枝驚鵲，清風半夜鳴蟬。
稻花香裏說豐年，聽取蛙聲一片。

七八個星天外，兩三點雨山前。
舊時茅店社林邊，路轉溪橋忽見。

Written to the tune "West River Moon" in the Shangrao area during the 1180s, with the note: "Traveling on the Huangsha Road at night" 夜行黃沙道中. This road was the section from Maodian Village 茅店村 to Huangsha Ridge, connecting the towns of Shangrao and Yanshan. The modest stone bridge is still there. The wine store, though, is gone.

51 Startled by the Moon a Magpie Took Off

Startled by the moon a magpie took off
cicadas droned in the chilly night air
the scent of flowering rice promised a good harvest
I stopped to listen to the frogs

A handful of stars in the sky
a few misty mountains ahead
the old wine store by the sacred grove
where the road turned I suddenly saw the bridge

52 句裏春風正剪裁

句裏春風正剪裁，溪山一片畫圖開。
輕歐自趁虛船去，荒犬還迎野婦回。

松共竹，翠成堆。
要擎殘雪鬬疏梅。
亂鴉畢竟無才思，時把瓊瑤蹴下來。

Written to the tune "Partridge Sky" in the Shangrao area during the 1180s, with the note: "Sights on the Huangsha Road" 黃沙道中即事.

52 I've Pieced Together Some Lines from Spring

I've pieced together some lines from spring
unrolled a painting of a mountain and river
weightless gulls chasing empty boats
scruffy dogs welcoming a village woman home

Bamboo and pines
hills turning green
traces of snow teasing the last plum blossoms
until a gaggle of crows with no sense of wonder
kick a crystalline shower to the ground

53 千峯雲起

千峯雲起，驟雨一霎時價。
更遠樹斜陽，風景怎生圖畫。
青旗賣酒，山那畔別有人家。
只消山水光中，無事過這一夏。

午醉醒時，松窗竹戶，萬千瀟灑。
野鳥飛來，又是一般閒暇。
卻怪白鷗，覷着人欲下未下。
舊盟都在，新來莫時，別有說話。

Written to the tune "Ugly Servant Prelude" during the 1180s, with the note: "On the Boshan Road in the style of Li Yi'an [Li Qingzhao]" 博山道中效李易安體. Li Qingzhao 李清照 was another of China's great lyric poets, certainly its most famous female exemplar. Xin Qiji refers to Liezi's story about the ability of seagulls to sense aggressive thoughts in people (*Liezi* 2.11). Hence he has made his own agreement with gulls to do no harm. Xin began referring to his agreement with the birds as early as 1182. See poem 25.

53 Clouds Rising from a Thousand Peaks

Clouds rising from a thousand peaks
the briefest of downpours
distant trees in the setting sun
how to paint such a scene
and a wine store's blue flags
where others on the mountain live
in such a landscape
I could spend all summer doing nothing

Waking at noon after drinking
bamboo and pines out my door and every window
countless forms of freedom
birds flying past
other worlds of leisure
I chastised the gulls
seeing me and about to land and not landing
despite our old agreement
it was different this time
as if they were trying to tell me something

54 今來何處

今來何處，有我愁，何處還知吾樂。
一點淒涼千古意，獨倚西風廖廓。
並竹尋泉，和雲種樹，喚做真閑客。
此心閑處，未應長藉丘壑。

休說往事皆非，而今云是，且把清尊酌。
醉裏不知誰是我，非月非雲非鶴。
露冷松梢，風高桂子，醉了還醒卻。
北窗高臥，莫教啼鳥驚著。

To the tune "Recalling a Pretty Girl" in the 1180s, with the note: "Written at Yuyan Cliff and in the style of Zhu Xizhen" 賦雨巖，效朱希真體. Zhu, aka Zhu Dunru 朱敦儒, was a minor Song poet. The north window is the last to brighten in the morning.

54 Where Lately

Where lately
are my sorrows
and where exactly are my joys
feeling the chill of a thousand generations
I let the vastness of the west wind take me
into the bamboo to find a spring
into the clouds to plant a tree
for I am truly an idle man
and this idle mind of mine
doesn't necessarily need a hill or valley

Don't tell me the past is all wrong
and the present is right
for that I turn to whiskey
when I'm drunk I don't know who I am
I'm not the moon or a cloud or a crane
the cold dew at the top of a pine
or a cassia tree in the wind
eventually I become sober
but while I'm sleeping below the north window
please don't wake the birds

55 枕簟溪堂冷欲秋

枕簟溪堂冷欲秋，斷雲依水晚來收。
紅蓮相倚渾入醉，白鳥無言定自愁。

書咄咄，且休休，一丘一壑也風流。
不知筋力衰多少，但覺新來懶上樓。

Written to the tune "Partridge Sky" in 1186 or 1187 in Shangrao, with the note: "Written upon becoming ill after returning from Ehu" 鵝湖歸, 病起作. The structure Xin Qiji refers to as his "river house" was located along the river that formed Daihu Lake just outside Shangrao's north gate. It was one of the main structures on his property. Ehu Lake, with its Buddhist temple and Confucian academy, was twenty kilometers southwest of Shangrao and one of Xin Qiji's favorite destinations.

55 Sleeping at My River House I Felt the Fall Air

Sleeping at my river house I felt the fall air
the clouds disappeared at dusk downstream
leaning on one another the lotuses looked drunk
the herons stood silent lost in thought

Scribbling about my sorrows
yet happy for the moment
every hill and valley has its charm
I didn't realize how weak I had become
lately I've discovered I can't climb stairs

56 誰向椒盤簪綵勝

誰向椒盤簪綵勝，整整韶華，爭上春風鬢。
往日不堪重記省，為花長把新春恨。

春未來時借問，晚恨開遲，早又飄零近。
今歲花期消息定，只愁風雨無憑準。

To the tune "A Butterfly's Favorite Flower," with the note: "Written at a party on the first day of spring in the Wushen Year [1188]" 戊申元日立春席間作. In addition to pepper—for adding to rice wine—the tray that people passed around to family members and guests on the first day of the year included papercuts of flowers, which were meant for decorating one's house or windows—not necessarily one's hair. The Chinese had something similar to a farmer's almanac with a calendar forecasting the coming seasons of the year.

56 Who Flaunts the Pepper Tray's Papercuts

Who flaunts the pepper tray's papercuts
only the truly young
vying to display spring in their hair
unwilling to reflect on the past
adding new regrets over flowers

Before every spring I worry
if the flowers are late I'll hate waiting
if they're early they'll be gone too soon
this year the season is now official
I just worry the wind and rain can't be trusted

57 莫折荼蘼

莫折荼蘼，且留取一分春色。
還記得青梅如豆，共伊同摘。
少日對花渾醉夢，而今醒眼看風月。
恨牡丹笑我倚東風，頭如雪。

榆筴陳，菖蒲葉。
時節換，繁華歇。
算怎禁風雨，怎經鶗鴂。
老冉冉兮花共柳，是栖栖者蜂和蝶。
也不因春去有閑愁，因離別。

To the tune "Whole River Red" in the spring of 1188 in Shangrao, with the note: "Another poem after entertaining Zheng Hengzhou at a party" 餞鄭衡州厚卿席上再賦. Zheng was heading south, off to serve in Hengzhou on the Xiang River. Peonies form their flower buds at the end of spring but don't bloom until the beginning of summer. Elm seedpods, or samaras, and iris leaves are also among the signs that spring is ending and summer about to begin. The cuckoo not only announces the end of spring; to the Chinese its plaintive call sounds like "better go home" 不如歸去—especially to those on the road or living in exile.

57 Don't Pick That Raspberry Flower

Don't pick that raspberry flower
leave it as a sign of spring
do you still remember those tiny green plums
you and I picked
when we were boys and drunk on flowers
sober now we prefer the moon and night air
and hate the peonies for mocking our attachment to the east wind
with our heads like snow

Elm tree samaras
and iris leaves
the seasons are changing
the flowering about done
how will we endure the wind and the rain
or survive the cuckoo's call
flowers and willows are so feeble
bees and butterflies so restless
it's not spring's departure that makes me sad
it's yours

58 醉裏挑燈看劍

醉裏挑燈看劍，夢回吹角連營。
八百里分麾下炙，五十絃翻塞外聲。
沙場秋點兵。

馬作的盧飛快，弓如霹靂弦驚。
了卻君王天下事，贏得生前身後名。
可憐白髮生。

Written to the tune "Interruption" in 1188, or shortly thereafter, following Xin Qiji's discussions with Chen Tongfu at Ehu, with the note: "I've written a heroic tune for Chen Tongfu and sent it to him" 為陳同甫賦壯詞以寄之. Chen Tongfu (d. 1194), or Chen Liang, was a famous opponent of Zhu Xi in discussions of neo-Confucian philosophy at what became the Ehu Academy. Eight Hundred Miles was a famous ox. Upon hearing the fifty-string zither, an emperor ordered it destroyed for being too sorrowful and limited the instrument to twenty-five strings. Dilu was the famous horse that carried Liu Bei to safety during a battle.

58 I Hold up a Lantern to Inspect My Sword When I'm Drunk

I hold up a lantern to inspect my sword when I'm drunk
dream of blowing a horn to wake the whole camp
dream I'm sharing the meat of Eight Hundred Miles
playing borderland tunes on a fifty-string zither
reviewing troops in fall in the dunes

A horse as fast as Dilu
a bow whose string snaps like lightning
deeds that complete our lord's great task
a name that lasts more than a lifetime
the appearance alas of white hair

59 三三兩兩誰家女

三三兩兩誰家女，聽取鳴禽枝上語。
提壺沽酒已多時，婆餅焦時須早。

醉中忘卻來時路，借問行人家住處。
只尋古廟那邊行，更過溪南烏桕樹。

Written to the tune "Jade Tower Spring" around 1189 at his Piaoquan Spring property, thirty kilometers southwest of Shangrao. The conversation here is among the birds. The river was the Qisi 期思, which was once spanned by a stone bridge not far from the spring. The directions are from the east side of the bridge to his house on the west side near the spring.

59 Who Are These Daughters in Twos and Threes

Who are these daughters in twos and threes
listening to the birds talking in the trees
Jug Carrier went for wine hours ago
Burnt Cookie left even earlier

Being drunk I forgot how I got there
I asked a passerby the way home
Just head for the old temple in that direction
it's across the river south of the tallow tree

60 剛者不堅牢

剛者不堅牢，柔底難摧挫。
不信張開口角看，舌在牙先墮。

已闕兩邊廂，又豁中間個。
說與兒曹莫笑翁，狗竇從君過。

Written to the tune "Master Diviner" around 1189, with the note: "A tooth fell out" 齒落. This was not the only poem Xin Qiji wrote this year about a tooth falling out. He was forty-nine. I wouldn't be surprised if making an opening for the family dog to come and go dates back to Neolithic times.

60 What's Hard Doesn't Last

What's hard doesn't last
what's soft seldom breaks
look in your mouth if you don't believe me
your tongue is there but your teeth are gone

I'm already missing two on the sides
also one in the middle
I told my boys don't laugh at your old man
you're welcome to use the doggie door

61 松岡避暑

松岡避暑，茆簷避雨，閑去閑來幾度。
醉扶怪石看飛泉，又卻是前回醒處。

東家娶婦，西家歸女，燈火門前笑語。
釀成千頃稻花香，夜夜費一天風露。

Written to the tune "Magpie Bridge Immortal" at his Daihu Lake residence, with the note: "Writing about something I saw while hiking in the mountains in the Jiyou Year [1189]" 己酉山行書所見.

61 To a Pine-Covered Ridge to Escape the Heat

To a pine-covered ridge to escape the heat
and a thatched hut to escape the rain
I've wandered back and forth countless times
once clung to a strange rock to see a waterfall
that was where I sobered up last time

A married woman in the lane
a daughter-in-law next door
laughing by their doors in the lamplight
a thousand acres of rice flowers turned into wine
sampling it every night with the windblown dew

62 聽我尊前醉後歌

聽我尊前醉後歌，人生無奈別離何。
但使情親千里近，須信，無情對面是山河。

寄語石頭城下水，居士，而今渾不怕風波。
借使未成鷗鳥伴，經慣，也應學得老漁蓑。

Written to the tune "Calming the Wind and Waves" in 1189 in Shangrao, with the note: "At a party seeing off Fan Kuozhi [Fan Kai 范開], who was on his way to Jian-kang" 席上送範廓之遊建康. Jiankang (Nanjing) was nearly five hundred kilometers from Shangrao. The journey would have been by boat via the Xinjiang River and Poyang Lake and finally the Yangzi. "Rock City" was an old name for Jiankang. Xin calls himself an "uncapped scholar" because he never passed the exams required for entry into the higher posts of bureaucracy. The expression "wind and waves," especially when used by poet-officials, usually refers to the vicissitudes in the court's appreciation of their talents. The fisherman in the last line is the one immortalized in the poem "River Snow" by Liu Zongyuan 柳宗元: "An old man in his raincoat in a solitary boat / fishes alone in the freezing river snow." It was Fan Kai who published the first collection of Xin Qiji's poems in 1188. When three more volumes were added, the collection became known as the Jiaxuan Four Folio Edition 稼軒四卷本, as opposed to the Xin Qiji Twelve Folio Edition 辛棄疾十二卷本 published after Xin's death.

62 Hear My After-I've-Been-Drinking Song

Hear my after-I've-been-drinking song
what can you do about parting
treat distant friends you love as nearby
trust me
and those nearby you don't love as mountains and rivers

I'm sending this to the water below the Rock City wall
this uncapped scholar
no longer fears the wind and waves
even if I hadn't become friends with the gulls
their confidant
I'd rather be a fisherman in a raincoat

63 日月如磨蟻

日月如磨蟻，萬事且浮休。
君看簷外江水，滾滾自東流。
風雨瓢泉夜半，花草雪樓春到，老子已菟裘。
歲晚問無恙，歸計橘千頭。

夢連環，歌彈鋏，賦登樓。
黃雞白酒，君去村社一番秋。
長劍倚天誰問，夷甫諸人堪笑，西北有神州。
此事君自了，千古一扁舟。

Written to the tune "Water Music Song" in 1189 or 1190, with the note: "Seeing off Yang Minzhan" 送楊民瞻. Piaoquan Spring was the name of a large parcel of land Xin Qiji bought in 1186. In 1195, when his residence at Daihu Lake burned down, he and his family moved to Piaoquan Spring, where he already had built a secondary residence. Snow Hall was a building Xin used for entertaining guests at his Daihu residence. It was named after Su Dongpo's study in Huangzhou. A man named Li Heng 李衡 once arranged for someone to plant a thousand orange trees and told his son that this would be his inheritance. Although everyone scoffed, the son became wealthy as a result. Emperors often presented linked jade disks to their favorite court officials, representing their unbreakable bond. Towers in China were built not only for the view; they were also used for practicing the Daoist art of droning 長嘯 to generate *qi*. The boat story is about Fan Li 范蠡, the prime minister of the ancient state of Yue. After he had helped his king conquer his enemies, Fan left in a boat and disappeared, only to reappear, to amass another fortune, and to once more disappear. One's life at court in ancient China often hung by a thread. The story is meant to remind Yang that even if he can succeed in reclaiming the lost lands, he should prepare an escape plan.

63 Like Ants on a Millstone Every Day Every Month

Like ants on a millstone every day every month
everything we do is ephemeral
you've seen the river beyond the eaves
wave after wave flowing east
the rain at Piaoquan Spring at midnight
plants at Snow Hall flowering in early spring
an old man with a place in mind
and no portents for your remaining years
your retirement plan a thousand orange trees

Dreaming about jade disks
you sing and beat your sword
write poems about climbing towers
or fat chickens and clear liquor
spend your autumns at the village shrine
where no one asks the name of your sword
and no one laughs that it's Heaven's Will
as for our sacred lands in the north
regarding that I know you know
the ancient tale about the boat

64 夜月樓臺

夜月樓臺，秋香院宇，笑吟吟地人來去。
是誰秋到便淒涼，當年宋玉悲如許。

隨分杯盤，等閒歌舞，問他有甚堪悲處。
思量卻也有悲時，重陽節近多風雨。

To the tune "Walking on Nutgrass," with the note: "Written two evenings after Mid-Autumn of the Gengxu Year [1190] at a small party on Zhuan Ridge at Daihu Lake" 庚戌中秋後二夕帶湖篆岡小酌. Zhuan Ridge formed the eastern border of Xin's estate. Song Yu (d. 222 BCE) was a shamanic poet who followed in the tradition of Qu Yuan (d. 278 BCE). Many of his poems, like Qu Yuan's, were preserved as part of the *Chuci* 楚辭 (Songs of Chu). The ninth day of the ninth month has long been celebrated by men in China as a time to congratulate themselves on living another year—nine being the ultimate *yang* number.

64 Moonlit Nights at the Pavilion

Moonlit nights at the pavilion
autumn-scented courtyards
people laughing coming and going
why get upset when fall arrives
in the past Song Yu was like that

Despite the wine and the food
no matter who sang or who danced
when asked what made him sad
he was sad just thinking
as Double Ninth approached that it might rain

65 倘來軒冕

倘來軒冕，問還是，今古人間何物。
舊日重城愁萬里，風月而今堅壁。
藥籠功名，酒壚身世，可惜蒙頭雪。
浩哥一曲，座中人物三傑。

休歎黃菊凋零，孤標應也有，梅花爭發。
醉裡重揩西望眼，惟有孤鴻明滅。
萬事從教，浮雲來去，枉了衝冠髮。
故人何在，長庚應伴殘月。

Written to the tune "Recalling a Pretty Girl" in 1191, with the note: "Getting drunk at Piaoquan Spring and matching Su Dongpo's rhyme" 瓢泉酒酣，和東坡韻. Su Dongpo was one of the first Song poets to explore and master the lyric form of poetry. Although Xin bought the land at Piaoquan Spring in 1186 and constructed a simple residence, he didn't move there permanently until 1195. A carriage and a starched hat were the standard accoutrements of officials who served at court.

65 If Somehow I Had a Carriage and Tall Hat

If somehow I had a carriage and tall hat
I would still have to ask
what such things were for
in towns once filled with sorrow
the wind and moon now guard the walls
despite having reached the inner circle
I spend my days in wineshops
my head covered with snow
singing songs out loud
to my fellow heroes

Why bemoan the withering of chrysanthemums
rarer examples exist
like plum buds struggling to bloom
when I'm drunk I wipe my eyes and look west
a lone goose appears then is gone
I'm letting everything go
all the passing clouds
getting angry would be a waste
where are my old friends
Venus still keeps the crescent moon company

66 長恨復長恨

長恨復長恨，裁作短歌行。
何人為我楚舞，聽我楚狂聲。
余既滋蘭九畹，又樹蕙之百畝，秋菊更餐英。
門外滄浪水，可以濯吾纓。

一杯酒，問何似，身後名。
人間萬事，毫髮常重泰山輕。
悲莫悲生離別，樂莫樂新相識，兒女古今情。
富貴非吾事，歸與白鷗盟。

To the tune "Water Music Song," with the note: "Written at a dinner with Chen Ruiren in Sanshan after being assigned there in the Renzi Year [1192]" 壬子三山被召，陳瑞仁給事飲餞席上作. Sanshan was another name for Fuzhou, where Xin was serving as magistrate as well as judicial commissioner of Fujian province. During the Han dynasty, ballads were divided into "short" and "long." The ancient kingdom of Chu 楚 occupied the middle reaches of the Yangzi. In the first stanza, lines 5 and 6 are from Qu Yuan's "Beset by Sorrow," and lines 8 and 9 from his "Yu Fu" 漁父 ("The Fisherman"), in which those who go to serve at court wash their hat strings, in Qu's case in the Canglang River 滄浪, while those who choose not to go wash their feet. The Mad Man of Chu's song to Confucius ended, "Those who seek to serve endanger themselves" (*Lunyu* 18.6).

66 My Never-Ending Everlasting Regrets

My never-ending everlasting regrets
I've reduced to a short ballad
someone show me a Chu-style dance
hear me become the Mad Man of Chu
I've cultivated whole hillsides of orchids
slopes of cymbidiums too
I've tasted chrysanthemum petals in fall
in the Canglang River beyond my door
I've washed my hat strings

A cup of wine
doesn't compare
to a name that survives death
in the course of doing all that we do
our white hair outweighs Mount Tai
nothing is more painful than leaving this life
nothing a greater pleasure than meeting a new friend
or the timeless love between a man and woman
wealth and fame don't interest me
I'm going home to be with my seagull friends

67 日日過西湖

日日過西湖，冷浸一天寒玉。
山色雖言如畫，想畫時難邈。

前弦後管夾歌鍾，才斷又重續。
相次藕花開也，幾蘭舟飛逐。

Written to the tune "Something Good Prelude" during Xin Qiji's stay in Fuzhou, 1192–1194, with the note: "At West Lake" 西湖. This was not the West Lake in Hangzhou, or the one in Yanshan.

67 It Drifts past West Lake Day After Day

It drifts past West Lake day after day
the cold aloof jade sky
people say these mountains are like a painting
I can't imagine such a painting

Strings then flutes then an interlude of bells
stopping then beginning again
lotuses taking turns blooming
painted boats flying by

68 莫望中州歎黍離

莫望中州歎黍離，元和聖德要君詩。
老去不堪誰似我，歸臥，青山活計費尋思。

誰築詩墻高十丈，直上，看君斬將更搴旗。
歌舞正濃還有語，記取，鬚髯不似少年時。

Written to the tune "Calming the Wind and Waves" in 1193 in Fuzhou, with the note: "A rhyme I've used before. Guohua provided the wine, and we sang and danced all night" 再用韻. 時國華置酒, 歌舞甚盛. Xin Qiji was still serving as magistrate of Fuzhou but was now also military commissioner of Fujian province. Guohua was the sobriquet of Lu Yande 盧彥德, who had replaced Xin as judicial commissioner of the province. This is the second of two poems Xin wrote for him. Xin Qiji is likening the times when he wrote this poem to the Yuanhe 元和 reign (806–820) of Emperor Xian 憲帝 of the Tang dynasty. When royal forces suppressed a separatist movement in the same region later occupied by the Jurchens in Xin's lifetime, the Tang poet Han Yu 韓愈 (d. 824) wrote a poem in celebration of their victory.

68 Don't Look Toward Our Lands and Sigh About Our Loss

Don't look toward our lands and sigh about our loss
we need your poems in these Yuanhe times
people old and inept like me
go home and lie down
thinking about a job in the mountains is a waste

If you can build a wall of poems a hundred feet high
put one up
I saw you raise our banner again
you sang and danced and said something profound
but I noticed
your beard isn't like when you were young

69 好雨當春

好雨當春，要趁歸耕。
況而今，已是清明。
小窗坐地，側聽簷聲。
恨夜來風，夜來月，夜來雲。

花絮飄零，鶯燕丁寧。
怕妨儂湖上閒行。
天心肯後，費甚心情。
放霎時陰，霎時雨，霎時晴。

Written to the tune "Offering Incense" in 1194, with the note: "Written in Sanshan" 三山作. Sanshan was an old name for Fuzhou. Xin's poem uses the scene at hand to comment on the vicissitudes of court politics—and the court's attitude toward him. "Heaven" refers to the emperor.

69 A Good Rain and a Proper Spring

A good rain and a proper spring
time to hurry home and plow
more importantly
it's Purification Day
sitting by my little window
listening to the rain
how I hate when the wind comes at night
when the moon comes at night
when the clouds come at night

As petals fly by
and orioles and swallows chatter
I worry this might stop my lakeside strolls
unless Heaven relents
but why confound my heart
let it be suddenly cloudy
suddenly rainy
suddenly clear

70 綠漲連雲翠拂空

綠漲連雲翠拂空。
十分風月處，着衰翁。
垂楊影斷岸西東。
君恩重，教且種芙蓉。

十里水晶宫。
有時騎馬去，笑兒童。
殷勤卻謝打頭風。
船兒住，且醉浪花中。

Written to the tune "Little Scarp" in 1194 in Fuzhou, with the note: "In Sanshan, boating with guests on West Lake" 三山與客泛西湖. The shore of the lake was lined with the palatial dwellings of the city's well-to-do. Despite his titles as magistrate of the city and military commissioner of the province, Xin had nothing better to do than go boating.

70 The Water and the Clouds Painted the Sky Green

The water and the clouds painted the sky green
a perfect place for the wind and moon
I'm a man affected by old age
and the reflection of willows along the shore
our lord was so kind
telling us to plant lotuses

Crystal palaces stretching for miles
riders racing by
children laughing
we actually thanked the headwind
our boat at anchor
drunk among the waves

71 老來曾識淵明

老來曾識淵明，夢中一見參差是。
覺來幽恨，停觴不御，欲歌還止。
白髮西風，折腰五斗，不應堪此。
問北窗高臥，東籬自醉，應別有，歸來意。

須信此翁未死，到如今凜然生氣。
吾儕心事，古今長在，高山流水。
富貴他年，直饒未免，也應無味。
甚東山何事，當時也道，為蒼生起。

Written to the tune "Water Dragon Song" in 1194 in Fuzhou, shortly before Xin followed Tao Yuanming's example by quitting his job and returning to his home at Piaoquan Spring. Tao Yuanming preferred to sleep on the cooler north side of his house, and his favorite view was that of his garden and Lushan 廬山 to the east. "High Mountains" and "Flowing Water" were two classic tunes for the zither made famous by Yu Boya 俞伯牙 and his friend Zhong Ziqi 鍾子期. The tune titles became synonymous with the link between two people's hearts. "East Mountain" here refers to Xie An, who left his mountain home south of Shaoxing to serve as prime minister of the Eastern Jin dynasty, whose capital was Nanjing. As a result of his decision to join the fray, Xie was successful in protecting the Jin from attacks by the Former Qin dynasty in the north. Xie was one of Xin Qiji's heroes, and he hoped to follow his example.

71 I Didn't Meet Yuanming Until I Was Old

I didn't meet Yuanming until I was old
it was as if I saw him in a dream
sober with an unspoken sadness
he put his cup down
he was about to sing but stopped
his white hair in the autumn wind
bending at the waist for a salary
was clearly a mistake
I asked if besides sleeping below the north window
and drinking by the eastern fence
there was something more
to his decision to retire

I have to believe the old man hasn't died
his life has inspired us ever since
filling our hearts
in the past and today
with high mountains and flowing water
as for the allure of riches and honors
if we can't avoid them
we should treat them as meaningless
as for East Mountain
he too said
to help others

72 吾衰矣

吾衰矣，須富貴何時，富貴是危機。
暫忘設醴抽身去，未曾得米棄官歸。
穆先生，陶縣令，是吾師。

待葺個園兒名佚老。
更作個亭兒名亦好。
閒飲酒，醉吟詩。
千年田換八百主，一人口插幾張匙。
便休休，更說甚，是和非。

Written to the tune "Tallest Tower" in 1194 in Fuzhou, with the note: "I planned to quit and go home, but my 'pups' stopped me because the yield of our fields was insufficient, and so I wrote this poem to scold them" 吾擬乞歸，犬子以田產未置止我，賦此罵之. By "pups," Xin is referring to his sons. The first line is from the *Lunyu* 7.5, in which Confucius complains he has stopped dreaming of Zhougong 周公, the Duke of Zhou, on whom he tried to model himself. Gifts of sweet wine and rice were expected by those in favor. "Master Mu" refers to Mu Sheng 穆生 and "Magistrate Tao" to Tao Yuanming, both of whom quit their posts and retired when they felt slighted because their emoluments of sweet wine and glutinous rice, respectively, were not forthcoming. Xin resigned his own posts soon after he wrote this.

72 Alas My Decline

Alas my decline
when will I be rich and honored
be trapped by riches and honors
since they forgot my sweet wine I'm leaving
since I never got any rice I'm quitting
Master Mu
Magistrate Tao
they're my teachers

I'll fix up a garden and call it Old Age Rest
also a pavilion I'll call Good Enough
being retired I'll drink wine
and once I'm drunk I'll sing poems
as for my thousand-year-old fields with their eight hundred owners
and how many spoons I can put in my mouth
I'd better stop now
and say nothing more
about what's right and wrong

73 千古李將軍

千古李將軍，奪得胡兒馬。
李蔡為人在下中，卻是封侯者。

蕓草去陳根，筧竹添新瓦。
萬一朝家舉力田，舍我其誰也。

Written to the tune "Master Diviner" in 1194 after Xin resigned his posts in Fuzhou and returned to Piaoquan Spring, where he remained for the next nine years. Li Guang 李廣 was a famous general of the Han dynasty whose exploits against the Huns were legendary. Once when he was captured, he killed one of his captors and rode away on the man's horse, and yet he never received a fief. Meanwhile, his cousin, Li Cai, rose to the position of chief minister through trickery and was enfeoffed as one of the Three Dukes 三公. Xin Qiji isn't being completely sarcastic about his skill as a farmer being worthy of recognition. Jiaxuan, the name he took for himself upon his retirement, could be read to mean "Farmhouse" or "Farmer First." Meanwhile, despite his exploits on the battlefield, he suffered the same fate as Li Guang.

73 The Illustrious General Li

The illustrious General Li
stole a Hun's horse
Li Cai was a lesser man
yet he was enfeoffed as a lord

When I cut weeds I get rid of the roots
when I need a roof tile I split bamboo
if the court ever summons a farmer
who if not me

74 亂雲擾擾水潺潺

亂雲擾擾水潺潺。
笑溪山，幾時閑。
更覺桃源，人去隔仙凡。
萬壑千巖樓外雪，瓊作樹，玉為欄。

倦遊回首且加飡。
短篷寒，畫圖間。
見說嬌顰，擁髻待君看。
二月東湖湖上路，官柳嫩，野梅殘。

Written to the tune "River God" in 1195, with the note: "Seeing off Yuan Jizhi going home to Yuzhang" 送元濟之歸豫章—Yuzhang refers to Nanchang. Peach Spring was the name of Mister Wang's winery on Boshan. Wang's products included "the sage" and "the fool." The East Lake referred to here was the one in Nanchang.

74 Swirling Clouds and Babbling Water

Swirling clouds and babbling water
I laugh at mountains and streams
never at peace
when I woke up at Peach Spring again
you were gone but not the sage or the fool
outside there was snow on a thousand hills and valleys
trees made of crystal
fences of jade

Weary traveler heading home take care
your sampan looks cold
in a painting
I heard a frowning beauty
with coiled hair awaits you
on the road past East Lake in late spring
new willow catkins
the last plum blossoms

75 醉裏且貪歡笑

醉裏且貪歡笑，要愁那得工夫。
近來始覺古人書，信着全無是處。

昨夜松邊醉倒，問松我醉何如。
只疑松動要來扶，以手推松曰去。

Written to the tune "West River Moon" sometime in 1195–1200, while Xin lived at Piaoquan Spring, with the note: "Feeling inspired" 遣興.

75 I Try to Be Happy When I'm Drunk

I try to be happy when I'm drunk
it doesn't take any effort to be sad
lately I've found in the books of the ancients
there is nothing I trust

Last night collapsing next to a pine
I asked *How drunk would you say I am*
thinking it was trying to help me up
I gave it a shove and said *Amscray*

76 杯汝來前

杯汝來前，老子今朝，點檢形骸。
甚長年抱渴，咽如焦釜，於今喜睡，氣似奔雷。
汝說劉伶，古今達者，醉後何妨死便埋。
渾如此，歎汝於知己，真少恩哉。

更憑歌舞為媒，算合作人間鴆毒猜。
況怨無大小，生於所愛，物無美惡，過則為災。
與汝成言，勿留亟退，吾力猶能肆汝杯。
杯再拜，道麾之即去，招則須來。

Written to the tune "Spring-Soaked Garden" in 1196 at Piaoquan Spring, with the note: "About to give up drinking, I warned my wine cup not to come near me" 將止酒，戒酒杯使勿近. Liu Ling (d. 300) was one of the Seven Sages of the Bamboo Grove 竹林七賢. Like his fellow recluses, he lived in the Taihang Mountains 太行 north of the ancient capital of Luoyang. Known for staying drunk for months on end, Liu had a servant who followed him wherever he went with a jug of wine and a shovel. The jug was for providing wine on demand, the shovel for digging his grave should it be necessary.

76 Come Here Wine Cup

Come here wine cup
while this old man
reflects on his health
I've been thirsty so long
my throat is like a scorched wok
and today when I was sleeping
my breath sounded like thunder
you speak of Liu Ling
that sage of the past
ready to die and be buried when he drank
if that is what you think
I bemoan how you treat a friend
with so little sympathy

Song and dance are enticements too
in league with the poison of envy
there's no big or small when it comes to hate
it arises from what we love
nothing is beautiful or ugly
excess is what leads to disaster
let's settle this now
be gone and leave me be
I still have the strength to control you
bowing the cup replied
Wave and I go
call and I come

77 新葺茅簷次第成

新葺茅簷次第成，青山恰對小窗橫。
去年曾共燕經營。

病怯杯盤甘止酒，老倚香火苦翻經。
夜來倚舊管弦聲。

Written to the tune "Washing Silk in the River" in 1196, with the note: "Occasional piece at Piaoquan Spring" 飄泉偶作.

77 I Rebuilt My Thatched Hut in Stages

I rebuilt my thatched hut in stages
my tiny window now faces the mountains
I started work last year together with the swallows

I've given up snacks and wine due to illness
I've turned to burning incense and trying to read sutras
then last night I heard music again

78 疊嶂西馳

疊嶂西馳，萬馬回旋，衆山欲東。
正驚湍直下，跳珠倒濺，小橋橫截，缺月初弓。
老合投閑，天教多事，檢校長身十萬松。
吾廬小，在龍蛇影外，風雨聲中。

爭先見面重重，看爽氣朝來三數峰。
似謝家弟子，衣冠磊落，相如庭戶，車騎雍容。
我覺其間，雄深雅健，如對文章太史公。
新堤路，問偃湖何日，煙水濛濛。

Written to the tune "Spring-Soaked Garden" in 1196, with the note: "Written at Qi Hermitage on Lingshan before my Yanhu Lake home was finished" 靈山齊菴賦，時築偃湖未成. It seems that Xin Qiji never had enough places to live or hang out in. Here he is, building another residence, this one on Lingshan 靈山, just north of Shangrao. His house on Daihu Lake had burned down the previous year, and he had already built a number of buildings at Piaoquan Spring. The ridges and peaks Xin describes are those of Lingshan. During the Jin dynasty (266–420), the Xie family was known for elegant attire. Sima Xiangru (d. 117 BCE) was the most famous poet of the Han dynasty, and Sima Qian 司馬遷 (d. ca. 87 BCE) its most famous historian, whose description of Sima Xiangru's courtyard is quoted here.

78 Ridge upon Ridge Galloping West

Ridge upon ridge galloping west
ten thousand steeds turning their heads
peaks trying to go east
suddenly the rain poured down
pearls danced and splattered
on the little bridge that spanned the flood
bowed like a crescent moon
at my age I should be retired
but Heaven has been keeping me busy
inspecting the height of ten thousand pines
outside my hut
the shadows of twisted branches
inside the sound of windblown rain

I tried to see the ridges first
then the cool morning air on two or three peaks
like the Xie family sons
perfectly attired
or Xiangru's courtyard
his horses and carriage so stately
I felt like I was there
heroic and elegant
as if facing the Grand Historian
on the new dike road
I asked about Yanhu Lake
when would it vanish in the mist

79 何人半夜推山去

何人半夜推山去，四面浮雲猜是汝。
常時相對兩三峰，走遍溪頭無覓處。

西風瞥起雲橫度，忽見東南天一柱。
老僧拍手笑相夸，且喜青山依舊住。

Written to the tune "Jade Tower Spring" in 1196 at Piaoquan Spring, with the note: "Playful poem to clouds and mountains" 戲賦雲山. According to ancient Chinese cosmology, the sky was supported by eight mountains. During historical times, several contenders claimed the title of "southeast pillar." Since none of these were near where Xin was living, and since this is a playful poem, I presume he was referring to his friend Zhu Xi. Zhu grew up in the town of Wuyishan 武夷山, fifty kilometers southeast of Piaoquan Spring, and was living there at the time Xin wrote this poem.

79 Who Moved the Mountain Last Night

Who moved the mountain last night
seeing nothing but clouds I guess it was you
for the handful of peaks I invariably see
I searched along the stream in vain

Suddenly the west wind whisked the clouds away
the sky's southeast pillar all at once reappeared
an old monk clapped and laughed at this show
happy the mountain was in its old place

80 聽兮清珮瓊瑤些

聽兮清珮瓊瑤些。
明兮鏡秋毫些。
君無去此，流昏漲膩，生蓬蒿些。
虎豹甘人，渴而飲汝，寧猿猱些。
大而流江海，覆舟如芥，君無助，狂濤些。

路險兮山高些。
塊予獨處無聊些。
冬槽春盎，歸來為我，製松醪些。
其外芳芬，團龍片鳳，煮雲膏些。
古人兮既往，嗟予之樂，樂簞瓢些。

Written to the tune "Water Dragon Song" in 1196 at Piaoquan Spring, with the note: "Using the character *xie* 些 [meaningless here and acting as a bridge] and writing about Piaoquan Spring again, a song for friends. Since the rhyme suited them so well, my friends all emptied their cups" 用些語再題瓢泉, 歌以飲客, 聲韻甚諧, 客皆為之釂. The poem is addressed to Piaoquan Spring itself, asking it not to let its water leave the mountains to join the sea. Drinking water was sometimes stored in a trough for use in winter. Dragon-ball and phoenix-wing teas were famous in the Song dynasty.

80 Pure as the Sound of a Jade Pendant

Pure as the sound of a jade pendant
clear as the appearance of down on a mirror
please don't leave
and join the muddy flood
choked with weeds
man-eating tigers
prefer you when they're thirsty
you also quiet down the gibbons
eventually you could reach the sea
and capsize boats like mustard seeds
don't help
those wild waves

Roads are steep here and the mountains high
living alone what can I do
a trough in winter a jug in spring
come back and make me
pine-pollen wine
and sweet-smelling
dragon-ball and phoenix-wing
cloud-paste teas
the ancients are gone
and my pleasures alas
are a rice bucket and a gourd

81 轎兒排了

轎兒排了，擔兒裝了，杜宇一聲催起。
從今一步一回頭，怎睚得，一千餘里。

舊時行處，舊時歌處，空有燕泥香墜。
莫嫌白髮不思量，也須有，思量去裏。

Written to the tune "Magpie Bridge Immortal" in 1196 at Piaoquan Spring, with the note: "Seeing off Fenqing" 送粉卿行. Fenqing was a female entertainer Xin met elsewhere, most likely in Hangzhou—a thousand *li* away. Having come to stay with him, she was now heading home. To the Chinese, the cuckoo's call sounds like "better go home."

81 Your Sedan Chair Is Ready

Your sedan chair is ready
your luggage packed
the cuckoo is urging you to hurry
with every step a look back
how will you endure
a thousand more *li*

The places where you walked
the places where you sang
the swallows' scented mud falling in vain
don't doubt this old man will be thinking
or what will surely be
in his thoughts

82 幾箇輕鷗

幾箇輕鷗，來點破一泓澄綠。
更何處一雙鸂鶒，故來爭浴。
細讀離騷還痛飲，飽看脩竹何妨肉。
有飛泉日日供明珠，五千斛。

春雨滿，秧新穀。
閑日永，眠黃犢。
看雲連麥隴，雪堆蠶簇。
若要足時今足矣，以為未足何時足。
被野老相扶入東園，枇杷熟。

Written to the tune "Whole River Red" in 1196 or 1197, with the note: "Goings-on at my mountain home" 山居即事. "Beset by Sorrow" was Qu Yuan's famous lament about failing to lead his king on the path of beauty and righteousness. The silkworm frames were full of cocoons, ready for spinning into silk.

82 A Few Weightless Gulls

A few weightless gulls
were about to break through a sheet of transparent green
from out of nowhere two mandarin ducks
dove in first
I was reading "Beset by Sorrow" and drinking
having had my fill of bamboo shoots why not some meat
a nearby waterfall supplied me with pearls
five thousand barrelsful a day

It rained enough this spring
the seedlings are now rice
days off last forever
and the calves love to sleep
the wheat fields look like clouds
and silkworm frames like piles of snow
if I wanted enough today was enough
if it wasn't it won't ever be
a farmer waved for me to join him in his orchard
the loquats were ripe

83 莫笑吾家蒼壁小

莫笑吾家蒼壁小，稜層勢欲摩空。
相知惟有主人翁。
有心雄泰華，無意巧玲瓏。

天作高山誰得料，解嘲試倩揚雄。
君看當日仲尼窮。
從人賢子貢，自欲學周公。

Written to the tune "Immortal by the River" sometime in the 1190s, with the note: "Soon after I spread the news about my discovery of Green Wall, some visitors came to see it for themselves, thinking it might be like such sights as Jade Pile, Cool Gorge, Steep Cliff, or Rock Chime. Upon seeing that it was only exceptional in terms of its height, they laughed and left. I thought I would have some fun with this and have responded here to their ridicule" 蒼壁初開, 傳聞過實, 客有來觀者, 意其如積翠, 清風, 巖石, 玲瓏之勝, 既見之, 乃獨為是突兀而止也, 大笑而去. 主人戲下一轉語, 為蒼壁解嘲. The other mountains cited here were also in what is now Yanshan county. Mount Tai and Mount Hua are two of China's five sacred mountains—four of which overlooked the Yellow River. The mountain he calls Green Wall was on his property. Hence Xin Qiji was, at that time, its owner. Yang Xiong 揚雄 was a philosopher of the Han dynasty, among whose compositions was "Response to Mockery" 解嘲. When Confucius and his disciples were traveling and without food, a disciple asked if a superior person should also suffer hardship. Confucius said, "Of course, but they endure hardship, while the inferior person engages in unlicensed behavior" (*Lunyu* 15.1). Zigong 子貢 was said to have been more virtuous than his teacher, Confucius, who modeled himself on Zhougong (the Duke of Zhou), who helped his father and brother found the Zhou dynasty. The duke was also responsible for initiating the rituals used at court and for establishing the concept of the "superior man," who takes part in them and thereby maintains the harmony of Man with Heaven and Earth. Another innovation of his was the concept of the Mandate of Heaven, whereby deposing the Son of Heaven was seen as justified when an emperor lost the support of Heaven through his unrighteous acts. Although the Chinese characters for "gong" here differ, Xin Qiji indulges himself with a play on words involving the names Zigong and Zhougong.

83 Don't Make Fun of This Green Wall of Mine

Don't make fun of this Green Wall of mine
its towering form nearly touches the sky
no one understands it except for its owner
its heart is heroic like Mount Tai or Mount Hua
to be exquisite like Rock Chime wasn't its intent

Who knows why Heaven made such a mountain
Yang Xiong has an answer for those who would mock it
consider when Confucius had nothing to eat
his disciple Zigong was more virtuous
but the Master was a student of Zhougong

84 欲行且起行

欲行且起行，欲坐重來坐。
坐坐行行有倦時，更枕閑書臥。

病是近來身，懶是從前我。
靜掃飄泉竹樹陰，且恁隨緣過。

Written to the tune "Master Diviner" around 1198 at Piaoquan Spring.

84 If I Feel Like Walking I Get Up and Walk

If I feel like walking I get up and walk
if I feel like sitting I sit down
whenever I get tired of sitting or walking
I lie in bed and read

Illness has lately been my lot
before that I was basically lazy
just clearing shady spots in the bamboo at Gourd Spring
that is how I've been spending my time

85 剩欲讀書已懶

剩欲讀書已懶，只因多病長閑。
聽風聽雨小窗眠，過了春光太半。

往事如尋去鳥，清愁難解連環。
流鶯不肯入西園，去喚畫梁飛燕。

Written to the tune "West River Moon" sometime between 1195 and 1200 at Piaoquan Spring, with the note: "Late spring" 晚春. Painted rafters were common in Buddhist and Daoist temples as well as the homes of the well-to-do.

85 I'd Like to Read but I'm Sleepy

I'd like to read but I'm sleepy
since becoming ill I just lie here
listening in bed to the wind and rain
spring more than half gone

Recalling the past is like tracking a bird
my regrets are like jade disks that can't be pulled apart
since orioles no longer visit my shaded garden
I called the swallows down from the painted rafters

86 走去走來三百理

走去走來三百理，五日以為期。
六日歸時已是疑，應是望多時。

鞭個馬兒歸去也，心急馬行遲。
不免相煩喜鵲兒，先報那人知。

Written to the tune "Wuling Spring" in the spring of 1200 at Piaoquan Spring. Xin Qiji wrote this for his friend Du Shilai 杜氏來 (aka Du Shugao 杜叔高), who had come to visit him that spring. The magpie was a symbol of a happy marriage, and the term was often used to refer to one's wife. Du's home was in Jinhua 金華, 160 kilometers to the northeast.

86 A Hundred Miles Here and Back

A hundred miles here and back
it's a five-day journey
after six someone must be wondering
no doubt watching the road

Better whip that horse and head home
hurry don't let it slow down
you can't help worrying that magpie
better send word so she'll know

87 百紫千紅過了春

百紫千紅過了春，杜鵑聲苦不堪聞。
却解啼教春小住，風雨，空出招得海棠魂。

恰似蜀宮當日女，無類，猩猩血染赭羅巾。
畢竟花開誰作主，記取，大都花屬惜花人。

Written to the tune "Calming the Wind and Waves" in the spring of 1200 at Piaoquan Spring. The cuckoo begins calling at the end of spring in China. To the Chinese, its call sounds like "better go home" *bu-ru gui-qu* 不如歸去. The Chinese gave it the same name they gave to rhododendrons and azaleas, which bloom at the end of spring. Xin elicits the bird and the flowers here. He uses the bird to summon the crabapple, which also blooms at the end of spring. Shu 蜀 was the kingdom that occupied the western half of what is now Sichuan 四川 province. It was founded around 1000 BCE by Du Yu 杜宇. Various stories are told about his retirement or death, which occurred in the second lunar month, when rhododendrons bloom and cuckoos begin calling. In one of these stories, the women in the palace, mourning his absence, dyed their scarves the color of the red rhododendron and started calling the cuckoo *du-juan* 杜鵑 instead of *zi-juan* 子鵑, using their absent lord's family name.

87 When Spring Ends with Its Countless Reds and Purples

When spring ends with its countless reds and purples
the rhody's sound is too painful to bear
trying to convince spring to stay longer
in the wind and rain
it summons the crabapple's soul in vain

Just like that time the Shu Palace women
without exception
dyed their scarves gibbon-blood red
when flowers bloom who is it really for
don't forget
flowers belong to flower lovers

88 案上數編書

案上數編書，非莊即老。
會說忘言始知道，萬言千句，不自能忘堪笑。
今朝梅雨霽，青天好。

一壑一丘，輕衫短帽。
白髮多時故人少，子雲何在，應有玄經遺草。
江河流日夜，何時了。

Written to the tune "Grateful for Royal Kindness" in the third month of 1200 at Piaoquan Spring, with the note: "While reading *Zhuangzi* and hearing that Zhu Huiyan (Zhu Xi) had died" 讀莊子聞朱晦菴即世. Xin Qiji's statement in the third line is a paraphrase of Zhuangzi's statement: "Words are used to convey ideas. Once you grasp the idea, you can forget the words" 言者所以在意, 得意而忘言. (*Zhuangzi* 26.11) Laozi said essentially the same thing in the first verse of his *Daodejing* 道德經: "The way that becomes a way / is not the Immortal Way / the name that becomes a name / is not the Immortal Name." The term "plum rains" refers to the rainy season in the southern half of China, which occurs in June and July, when plums ripen. Ziyun was the style name of the Han-dynasty philosopher Yang Xiong, to whom Xin Qiji is comparing his recently departed friend, Zhu Xi, the preeminent neo-Confucian philosopher of the Song dynasty. The reason Xin avoids using his friend's name here is that he didn't want to incur the wrath of the Song prime minister, Han Tuozhou, who banned any mention of Zhu Xi's ideas between 1195 and 1199 and even tried to have him executed. The text referred to here is Yang Xiong's *Taixuan* 太玄 (Great Mystery), which is used as a stand-in here to avoid mentioning Zhu Xi's famous commentary on the Confucian *Daxue* 大學 (Great Learning).

88 Of the Books on My Table

Of the books on my table
if it's not Laozi it's Zhuangzi
who says *To know the Way forget the words*
after thousands of words and countless expressions
funny how they couldn't forget themselves
this morning the plum rains stopped
the sky was perfectly clear

In the hills and valleys
he wore a light coat and simple cap
by the time we're old such friends are few
Ziyun is gone
but copies of his mystic text survive
great rivers flow night and day
they never stop

89 壯歲旌旗擁萬夫

壯歲旌旗擁萬夫，錦襜突騎渡江初。
燕兵夜娖銀胡騄，漢箭朝飛金僕姑。

追往事，歎今吾，春風不染白髭鬚。
卻將萬字平戎策，換得東家種樹書。

Written to the tune "Partridge Sky" in 1200 at Piaoquan Spring, with the note: "While I was enjoying talking with a visitor about our achievements and reputations, upon recalling the events of our youth, I wrote this for fun" 有客慨然談功名, 因追念少年時事, 戲作. The Southern Song dynasty was only able to protect itself from invasion by the Jin with a large and powerful navy, the construction of which denuded many of the mountains in the Yangzi watershed—hence the imperial orders to plant trees.

89 In the Prime of My Youth I Led Ten Thousand Men

In the prime of my youth I led ten thousand men
dressed in brocade we charged across the Yangzi
all night the Jurchens filled their silver quivers
we fitted our shafts with arrowheads of gold

Reflecting on the past
I sigh about who I've become
the spring wind can't dye my beard black again
all the plans I submitted for defeating our foes
have turned into orders from our lord to plant trees

90 昨日春如

昨日春如，十三女兒學繡。
一枝枝，不教花瘦。
甚無情，便下得，雨僝風僽。
向園林，鋪作地衣紅縐。

而今春似，輕薄蕩子難久。
記前時，送春歸後。
把春波，都釀作，一江醇酎。
約清愁，楊柳岸邊相候。

Written to the tune "Powdered Butterfly" around the year 1200, with the note: "Matching a poem published by Zhao Jinchen about falling plum blossoms" 和趙晉臣敷文賦落梅. Zhao Jinchen was Zhao Buyu 趙不迂, a prominent member of the court and in charge of the Hall for the Diffusion of Literature. Plum blossoms were usually white, but Zhongshan Mountain in Nanjing is still famous for its red blossoms.

90 Yesterday Was like Spring

Yesterday was like spring
thirteen girls learning embroidery
and on each branch
no shortage of flowers
how heartless
the sudden ravages of wind and rain
carpeting the orchard
with crimson brocade

Today is like spring too
amusements don't last
I recall the last time
after bidding the season goodbye
using the spring flood
to ferment
a river of nectar
and the sadness of our meeting
on the willow-lined shore

91 花向今朝粉面匀

花向今朝粉面匀，柳因何事翠眉顰。
東風吹雨細於塵。

自笑好山如好色，只今懷樹更懷人。
閒愁閒恨一番新。

Written to the tune "Washing Silk in the River" in 1200 at Piaoquan Spring after returning from an excursion, with the note: "Playful air on spending the night at a mountain monastery with Du Shugao and Wu Zisi" 偕杜叔高吳子似宿山寺戲作.

91 This Morning She Was Made Up like a Flower

This morning she was made up like a flower
so why the drooping willow-leaf eyebrows
the face powder damp from spring mist

I laugh about loving mountains as much as beauty
suddenly today a person more than a tree
but the sorrow and regret are something new

92 父老爭言雨水勻

父老爭言雨水勻，眉頭不似去年顰。
殷勤謝卻甑中塵。

啼鳥有時能勸客，小桃無賴已撩人。
梨花也做白頭新。

Written to the tune "Washing Silk in the River" in 1200 at Piaoquan Spring.

92 Old Men Argue Whether It Will Rain Enough

Old men argue whether it will rain enough
anxious to forget the dust in their pots
their brows aren't furrowed like last year

Bird songs can move an exile any time of year
peach buds are already a brazen tease
suddenly pear blossoms remind me of old men

93 君如九醞臺粘盞

君如九醞臺粘盞，我似茅柴風味短。
幾時秋水美人來，長恐扁舟乘興嬾。

高懷自飲無人勸，馬有青芻奴白飯。
向來珠履玉簪人，頗覺斗量車載滿。

Written to the tune "Jade Tower Spring" in 1200 at Piaoquan Spring, with the note: "Using this rhyme to reply to Deputy Magistrate Wu Zisi" 用韻答吳子似縣尉.

93 My Lord Is a Jade Cup of the Best Aged Wine

My lord is a jade cup of the best aged wine
I'm like dregs short on taste
will my friend ever visit these autumn waters
a boat trip I fear is beyond him

What I love most is to drink without a reason
for my horses to have fresh hay and my servants white rice
people who wear jeweled shoes and jade hairpins
lately I've noticed fill their carts to the railings

94 茅簷低小

茅簷低小，溪上青青草。
醉裡吳音相媚好，白髮誰家翁媼。

大兒鋤豆溪東，中兒正織雞籠。
最喜小兒無賴，溪頭臥剝蓮蓬。

Written to the tune "Peace and Purity" in the fall of 1200 at Piaoquan Spring, with the note: "Village life" 村居. The Wu 吳 dialect was spoken by people throughout the lower reaches of the Yangzi, especially in such towns as Suzhou, which was the capital of the ancient state of Wu.

94 A Thatched Hut

A thatched hut
a grass-lined stream
the charming slurred dialect of Wu
who is that white-haired couple

Their eldest son hoeing beans across the stream
their second son weaving cages for chickens
their spoiled utterly bored youngest son
lying beside the shore shelling lotus pods

95 甚矣吾衰矣

甚矣吾衰矣。
悵平生，交遊零落，只今餘幾。
白髮空垂三千丈，一笑人間萬事。
問何物，能今公喜。
我見青山多嫵媚，料青山，見我應如是。
情與貌，略相似。

一尊搔首東窗裏。
想淵明，停雲詩就，此時風味。
江左沈酣求名者，豈識濁醪妙理。
回首叫，雲飛風起。
不恨古人吾不見，恨古人，不見吾狂耳。
知我者，二三子。

Written to the tune "Congratulating the Bridegroom" in 1201 at Piaoquan Spring, with the note: "I wrote the lyrics to this tune for my garden pavilion. One day while sitting below Motionless Cloud enjoying the landscape, I thought the river and mountains wanted me to give them something, so I wrote a few lines, more or less resembling when Tao Yuanming was thinking about his friends" 邑中園亭, 僕皆為賦此詞. 一日獨坐停雲, 水聲山色, 競來相娛, 意溪山欲援例者, 遂作數語, 庶幾彷彿淵明思親友之意云. The first line is from the *Lunyu* 7.5. The pavilion was on a hill south of Xin's home. He borrowed the pavilion's name, and the first line of the second stanza, from Yuanming's poem "Motionless Clouds." "East Shore" refers to that of the Yangzi south of Nanjing, where revelries of the rich and powerful were frequent during Yuanming's lifetime. Yuanming preferred unfiltered wine, though he sometimes used his bandanna.

95 My Decline Has Been Extreme

My decline has been extreme
but what is sad about this life
is how friendships have withered
and so few remain
that and this mile of useless white hair
I laugh at the ten thousand things we do
and wonder which ones
we can enjoy now
the mountains look so lovely
I just hope the mountains
see me that way too
how I look and feel
as more or less the same

I was scratching my head and raising a cup at the east window
thinking about Yuanming
whether his poem about motionless clouds
felt like this
on East Shore they sought fame in bacchanals
ignorant of the wonder of unfiltered wine
I turned my head and yelled
for the wind to rise and clouds to fly
I don't regret not meeting the ancients
I regret the ancients
not meeting this madman
and those who know me
so few

96 北隴田高踏水頻

北隴田高踏水頻，西溪禾早已嘗新。
隔墻沽酒煮纖鱗。

忽有微涼何處雨，更無留影霎時雲。
賣瓜聲過竹邊村。

Written to the tune "Washing Silk in the River" in the late summer of 1203, with the note: "Sights on the Changshan Road" 常山道中即事. This road was between Shangrao and Quzhou 衢州. Xin Qiji was on his way to take up his new post as magistrate of Shaoxing—a half day's ride from the capital in Hangzhou. The prime minister, Han Tuozhou, was planning to resume military efforts against the Jurchens and wanted Xin close by when operations began. Xin and Han, however, did not get along well, and Xin returned home the following spring. To lift water to higher fields, farmers used a series of pedal-operated paddles. Minnows and small fish were often fried and eaten as a snack to accompany rice wine as well as stronger spirits.

96 The Pedaling Never Stops in the Terraced Fields to the North

The pedaling never stops in the terraced fields to the north
along streams to the west they're eating early rice
neighbors selling wine and frying tiny fish

It suddenly turned cool and was raining in all directions
a moment later not a trace of a cloud
a melon seller's call echoed beyond the bamboo

97 膠膠擾擾幾時休

膠膠擾擾幾時休，一出山來不自由。
秋水觀中山月夜，停雲堂下菊花秋。

隨緣道理應須會，過分功名莫強求。
先自一身愁不了，那堪愁上更添愁。

Written to the tune "Auspicious Partridge" in the fall of 1204 in Zhenjiang. Not long after returning home from Shaoxing in the spring of this year, Xin Qiji was once more called out of retirement. After an audience with Emperor Ningzong 寧宗, he was put in charge of the Zhenjiang (Jingkou) commandery, which guarded the entrance to the southern section of the Grand Canal leading to the capital in Hangzhou. Fall Flood Terrace and Motionless Cloud Pavilion were structures on his property at Piaoquan Spring. The name "Fall Flood Terrace" came from the title of chapter 17 of the *Zhuangzi* 莊子, in which the Lord of the North Sea corrects the limited awareness of the Lord of the Yellow River who, seeing the river in flood in fall, thinks it great—until he sees the water disappearing into the boundless sea. The name of the pavilion came from a series of four poems by Tao Yuanming.

97 The Turmoil and Confusion Never Stop

The turmoil and confusion never stop
since leaving the hills I can no longer choose
a moonlit night in the mountains at Fall Flood Terrace
or chrysanthemums in autumn below Motionless Cloud Pavilion

I should have learned the lesson of letting go
not fighting for more success and fame
my cares are already endless
what am I doing adding more

98 何處望神州

何處望神州，滿眼風光北固樓。
千古興亡多少事，悠悠。
不盡長江滾滾流。

年少萬兜鍪，坐斷東南戰未休。
天下英雄誰敵手，曹劉。
生子當如孫仲謀。

Written to the tune "Man from the South" in 1204 in Zhenjiang, with the note: "Thoughts on climbing Jingkou's Beigu Tower" 登京口北固有懷. Beigu Tower was built in honor of Sun Quan (Zhongmou), who died in 252. This is a poem extolling Sun's bravery in his battles against Cao Cao and Liu Bei; as the Han dynasty was ending, the three men vied with each other to succeed it. Xin was impressed with Sun's valor, as he always fought against greater forces. This would be Xin Qiji's final assignment, and he can't help but regret not having the opportunity once more to display the valor he did as a young man.

98 Where Can I Gaze on Our Sacred Lands

Where can I gaze on our sacred lands
from Beigu Tower the scenes fill my eyes
the rise and fall of so many generations
on and on
the relentless Yangzi flows on

Leading ten thousand men when he was young
guarding the southeast fighting without rest
which of the world's heroes was his equal
Cao Cao or Liu Bei
sons should be like Sun Zhongmou

99 悠悠萬世功

悠悠萬世功，矻矻當年苦。
魚自入深淵，人自居平土。

紅日又西沉，白浪長東去。
不是望金山，我自思量禹。

Written to the tune "Fresh Hawthorn Berries" in 1204 in Zhenjiang (Jingkou), with the note: "Inscribed at Jingkou commandery's Chenbiao Pavilion" 題京口郡治塵表亭. This pavilion no longer exists. Like Beigu Tower, it looked out upon the Yangzi, which Yu the Great (d. 2177 BCE) is said to have dredged so that its main stream could reach the sea and so that flooding of the delta region would cease. Until he succeeded, the world was in such disarray, the sun appeared to set in the east. From both Beigu Tower and Chenbiao Pavilion, the small island of Jinshan and its famous Buddhist monastery were visible just offshore.

99 The Endless Achievements of Countless Generations

The endless achievements of countless generations
the constant toil endured in those years
so fish could return to deep waters
so people could settle on the plains

The sun once again sets in the west
waves have ever since vanished in the east
it's not Jinshan I'm gazing upon
I'm thinking of Yu the Great

100 暮年不賦短長句

暮年不賦短長句，和得淵明數首詩。
君自不歸歸深易，今猶未足足何時。

偷閑定向山中老，此意須教鶴輩知。
聞道只今秋水上，故人曾榜北山移。

Written to the tune "Auspicious Partridge" in 1205 in Zhenjiang, with the note: "In Jingkou thinking of an old friend in the mountains" 京口有懷山中故人. Both Su Dongpo and Xin Qiji wrote *shi*-style poems that matched the rhyme schemes of Tao Yuanming. Tao's decision to retire from public service at the age of forty inspired others to do the same and embarrassed those who wished they could, which included Su Dongpo and Xin Qiji. It's no coincidence that both Su and Xin wrote poems matching the rhymes of Yuanming near the end of their lives. At the end of the first stanza, Xin paraphrases Laozi's *Daodejing* 46: "No disaster is greater than not knowing when you have enough." Fall Flood Terrace was one of the structures Xin Qiji built across the road from his Piaoquan Spring residence overlooking the Qisi River to the east. See the notes to poems 95 and 97. In poem 102, Xin Qiji refers to his friends "dawn gibbon" and "night crane" as genuine recluses. A writer named Kong Zhigui 孔稚珪 (d. 501) wrote an essay titled "North Hills Dispatch" in which he contrasted real recluses and frauds. The North Hills are the mountains outside the north wall of Nanjing, a favorite haunt of seekers of seclusion during the Six Dynasties. In his famous essay, Kong called on forest spirits to keep frauds from entering the mountains.

100 I've Stopped Writing Lyric Poems in Old Age

I've stopped writing lyric poems in old age
I've been matching the verses of Yuanming
it would be so easy for you to retire
if you haven't had enough when will you

Head for the mountains if you can get away
just make sure you let the crane and gibbon know
at Fall Flood Terrace I recently heard
an old friend has posted the "North Hills Dispatch"

101 江頭一帶斜陽樹

江頭一帶斜陽樹，總是六朝人住處。
悠悠興廢不關心，惟有沙洲雙白鷺。

仙人磯下多風雨，好卸征帆留不住。
直須抖擻盡塵埃，卻趁新涼秋水去。

To the tune "Jade Tower Spring," with this note: "Written in the Yichou Year [1205] after leaving the sacrificial temple at Jingkou [Zhenjiang] and heading west for home, just before reaching Immortal Rocks" 乙丑京口奉祠西歸，將至仙人磯. The scene is between the sandbars and rocky east shore of the Yangzi thirty kilometers south of Jiankang (Nanjing), where many of the rich and powerful had estates during the Six Dynasties period, when Jiankang was the capital of the southern half of China.

101 Trees at Sunset Along the River

Trees at sunset along the river
where people in the Six Dynasties once lived
oblivious of the endless rises and falls
a pair of egrets nest on the sandbar now

At Immortal Rocks due to the wind and rain
passenger boats don't stop anymore
I may as well shake off the dust
and ride the cool waters of autumn home

102 偶向停雲堂上坐

偶向停雲堂上坐，曉猿夜鶴驚猜。
主人何事太塵埃。
低頭還說向，被召又重來。

多謝北山山下老，殷勤一語佳哉。
借君竹杖與芒鞋。
徑須從此去，深入白雲堆。

Written to the tune "Immortal by the River" in the fall of 1205, with the note: "Casual poem at Motionless Cloud" 停雲偶作. The pavilion, to which Xin Qiji has returned, was on a hill just south of his home at Piaoquan Spring. "Dawn gibbon" and "night crane" were nicknames for reclusive friends. Based on his comments in poem 100, they were probably living in the hills near or on his estate. Following the essay "North Hills Dispatch" 北山移文 by Kong Zhigui, the expression "North Hills" became shorthand for a place where recluses lived. Of the lines in italics, the first and the last three are spoken by Xin's friends.

102 I Happened to Reach Motionless Cloud Pavilion

I happened to reach Motionless Cloud Pavilion
the dawn gibbon and night crane were surprised
Where did that dust come from
lowering my head I replied
I was called to court now I'm back

I thanked my friends down from the North Hills
for the earnestness of their words
Take this cane and these sandals
the trail begins here
to the land in the clouds

103 期思溪上日千回

期思溪上日千回，樟木橋邊酒數杯。
人影不隨流水去，醉顏重帶少年來。

疎蟬響澀林逾靜，冷蝶飛輕菊半開。
不是長卿終慢世，只緣多病又非才。

Written to the tune "Auspicious Partridge" in the fall of 1205 at Piaoquan Spring. Xin's residence was adjacent to the Qisi River, which was spanned by Camphor Tree Bridge. Although the old bridge is gone, the river is still there, as are several ancient camphor trees. Sima Xiangru was the most famous poet of the Han dynasty. Unlike Xin Qiji's earlier residence on Daihu Lake, his residence at Piaoquan Spring was more of a farming compound with a variety of dwellings and structures where he could enjoy different aspects of country living. Also, unlike Sima Xiangru before him, Xin had not given up hoping for an opportunity to help reclaim the dynasty's lost lands, having just returned from such an assignment in Zhenjiang, one that didn't work out.

103 On the Qisi River a Thousand Times a Day

On the Qisi River a thousand times a day
we drank cup after cup on Camphor Tree Bridge
our reflections not leaving with the water
our flushed faces bringing back younger days

When fewer cicadas drone the woods sound quieter
when fewer butterflies flutter chrysanthemums begin to bloom
I didn't renounce the world like Sima Xiangru
it's just that I'm ill and have no talents

104 萬事雲煙忽過

萬事雲煙忽過，百年蒲柳先衰。
而今何事最相宜，宜醉宜遊宜睡。

早趁催科了納，更量出入收支。
乃翁依舊管些兒，管竹管山管水。

Written to the tune "West River Moon" in 1207 at Piaoquan Spring, with the note: "For my sons, entrusting them with the family business" 示兒曹，以家事付之. The shore willow, or *Salix mesnyi,* grows near water and loses its leaves before other plants in the fall. Although Xin Qiji sensed his life approaching its end, he still didn't lose his sense of humor.

104 Everything Is Disappearing like Clouds or Smoke

Everything is disappearing like clouds or smoke
my vitality is withering faster than a shore willow's
what am I good at anymore
besides drinking visiting and sleeping

I've already turned over the taxes
also the income and expense accounts
meanwhile I'll continue to deal with the trifles
like mountains and rivers and bamboo

105 賢愚相去

賢愚相去，算其間能幾。
差以毫釐繆千里。
細思量義利，舜蹠之分，孳孳者，等是雞鳴而起。

味甘終易壞，歲晚還知，君子之交淡如水。
一餉聚飛蚊，其響如雷，深自覺昨非今是。
羨安樂窩中泰和湯，更劇飲，無過半醺而已。

To the tune "Cave Immortal Song" at Piaoquan Spring, with the note: "Written in the eighth month of the Dingmao Year [1207], while ill" 丁卯八月病中作. Xin Qiji died a month later. He is referring here to an old adage: "True friends don't have much to say. Their friendship is plain, like water." "Happy hideaway" and "cup of peace" were phrases used by the reclusive poet Shao Yong 邵雍 (d. 1077) to refer to a life of simplicity. When it came to wine, Shao Yong once said he never drank to get drunk, only enough to feel at peace.

105 Comparing Worthies and Fools

Comparing worthies and fools
how far apart are they
if a hair is the same as a thousand miles
carefully consider the just and the greedy
the difference between a sage and thief
equally diligent
they're both up at dawn

Sooner or later sweet things spoil
at the end of my life I finally know
true friendships are like water
rich meals attract bugs
their din like thunder
I know I was wrong in the past but not today
give me a happy hideaway and a cup of peace
no matter how much I drink
I won't get more than half-drunk

106 月明秋曉

月明秋曉，翠蓋團團好。
剪碎黃金教恁小，都著葉兒遮了。

折來休似年時，小窗能有高低。
無頓許多香處，只消三兩枝兒。

Undated and written to the tune "Peace and Purity," with the note: "Poem for a cassia tree" 賦木樨詞. Chinese people see, among other things, a cassia tree on the moon, beneath which a hare pounds the elixir of immortality. Wine infused with cassia flowers is often drunk during the Mid-Autumn festival. It was Su Dongpo's favorite wine.

106 On the Mid-Autumn Moon at Dawn

On the mid-autumn moon at dawn
the green canopy looks perfectly round
its tiny golden flowers so small
they're completely hidden by leaves

If I could pick some it would be like New Year
my little window would look so much better
I don't need a lot of perfume
two or three twigs would be fine

107 可憐今夕月

可憐今夕月，向何處，去悠悠。
是別有人間，那邊才見，光影東頭。
是天外空汗漫，但長風浩浩送中秋。
飛鏡無根誰繫，姮娥不嫁誰留。

謂經海底問無由，恍惚使人愁。
怕萬里長鯨，縱横觸破，玉殿瓊樓。
蝦蟆故堪浴水，問云何玉兔解沉浮。
若道都齊無恙，云何漸漸如鉤。

Undated and written to the tune "Magnolia Flower Lento," with the note: "Mid-Autumn and drinking wine until dawn—a guest said the poems people wrote in the past were meant to accompany the moon, not to the moon. This is why I've used the poetic form of Qu Yuan's 'Questions to Heaven'" 中秋飲酒將旦, 客謂前人詩詞有賦待月, 無送月者. 因用天問體賦. Heng'e (also Chang'e) is the goddess who lives on the moon. In the second stanza, Xin Qiji refers to an old Chinese legend that when the moon sets in the west, it goes under the sea before it reappears in the east. In addition to the hare, there is also a toad on the moon.

107 The Moon Is So Lovely Tonight

The moon is so lovely tonight
where is it going
wandering off
to another world
where someone else must have noticed
its light in the east
or beyond the sky into boundless space
where a much stronger wind sees autumn off
this flying mirror has no roots or tether
Heng'e never married so she can't be detained

But why would it sink beneath the sea as some claim
its faint light there would be sad
what if a whale a hundred miles long
accidentally destroyed
its jeweled tower or crystal palace
that would explain why toads take baths
but not why the jade hare can't swim
if you think its shape wouldn't be thereby diminished
why does it turn into a hook

108 困不成眠奈夜何

困不成眠奈夜何，情知歸未轉愁多。
暗將往事思量遍，誰把多情惱亂他。

些底事，誤人哪，不成真箇不思家。
嬌癡卻妒香香睡，喚起醒鬆說夢些。

Undated and written to the tune "Partridge Sky." Little Perfume (Xiangxiang) was the name of the woman's maid, who, in this case, was surely enjoying a better dream.

108 What Does She Do When She Can't Sleep at Night

What does she do when she can't sleep at night
knowing he's not back she worries
thinking about what happened in the past
him vexed by the charms of another

With such thoughts
she torments herself
not that he's not thinking of home
envious of Little Perfume sleeping so sweetly
she wakes her and asks about her dream

109 春動酒旗風

春動酒旗風，野店芳醪留客。
繫馬水邊幽寺，有梨花如雪。

山僧欲看醉魂醒，茗碗泛香白。
微記碧苔歸路，裊一鞭春色。

Undated and written to the tune "Something Good Prelude," with the note: "Spring day outing" 春日郊遊. During the Song, tea leaves were usually ground into a powder, then mixed with hot water and whipped into a froth. The custom disappeared in China but was preserved in Japan. I've heard this process is making a comeback in the Middle Kingdom, as one benefit is that you drink the ground leaves along with the brew. Then again, that might be why the Chinese switched to limiting themselves to the brew. The mention of "floating white perfume" could simply refer to the whipped tea but also suggests the presence of pear petals.

109 Spring Wind Was Blowing and a Wine Flag Was Flapping

Spring wind was blowing and a wine flag was flapping
the sweet mash of a country store detained us
we tied up our horses at a lakeside temple
the pear blossoms were like snow

A monk tried to sober us up
with cups of tea and floating white perfume
I vaguely recall the moss on the road home
waving my whip at spring scenes

110 看燈元是菩提葉

看燈元是菩提葉，依然會說菩提法。
法似一燈明，須臾千萬燈。

燈邊花更滿，誰把空花散。
說與病維摩，而今天女歌。

Undated and written to the tune "Bodhisattva Barbarian," with the note: "At a party with Zhao Jinchen when he brought out a bodhi-leaf lamp. Despite his illness, Zhao Maojia held it up and sang" 趙晉臣席上. 時張菩提葉燈, 趙茂嘉扶病攜歌者. Zhao Jinchen and Zhao Maojia were descendants of the founder of the Song dynasty and residents of Yanshan, just north of Piaoquan Spring. Both men were among Xin Qiji's closest friends and are mentioned in more than two dozen poems. The Sanskrit word *bodhi* means "enlightenment," and the Sanskrit word *dharma* means anything considered to be real or true. When capitalized it refers to the teaching of a buddha. Bodhi-leaf lanterns were popular in Hangzhou during the Song and were made of waxed paper to which were attached banyan leaves—similar to those of the tree beneath which Shakyamuni achieved enlightenment. When the candle inside the lantern was lit, the leaves cast flower-like shapes on walls and objects. In chapter 7 of the *Vimalakirti Sutra,* a deva appears in the room of the sick layman, Vimalakirti, and scatters flowers over everyone present. As they fall on the bodhisattvas (followers of the Mahayana path), they drop off and onto the floor. As they fall on Sariputra (follower of the Hinayana path), they stick to his clothing, and he is unable to shake them off. The deva then expounds the Dharma, or teaching of the Buddha, and when Sariputra understands, the flowers fall to the floor.

110 Look at This Lantern of Bodhi Leaves

Look at this lantern of bodhi leaves
teaching the Dharma of buddhahood
its light like the Dharma
lighting countless others

Surrounding the lantern is a world of flowers
who can shake off their phantom forms
instructing the invalid Vimalakirti
the deva is still singing today

111 態濃意遠

態濃意遠，眉顰笑淺，薄羅衣窄絮風軟。
鬢雲欺翠卷。

南園花樹春光暖。
紅香徑裏榆錢滿。
欲上鞦韆又驚懶，且歸休怕晚。

Undated and written to the tune "Drunken Peace," with the note: "Spring evening" 春晚. Women in China began pinching their eyebrows over two thousand years ago to emulate Xi Shi 西施, whose beauty, it was said, brought a kingdom to ruin. Little did the women realize Xi Shi's eyebrow malady was due to a heart condition. South Garden was located at the southeast corner of Hangzhou's West Lake and was the private garden of Prime Minister Han Tuozhou, with whom Xin had a strained relationship. The samaras, or seedpods, of elm trees looked like the metal coins used by the Chinese during the Tang and Song dynasties. The swing referred to here was not your ordinary swing. Swinging while sitting on a wooden board suspended on ropes thirty or more feet in length originated as part of the marriage customs of hill tribes in South China and was taken up by the Song nobility for entertainment. The implication here is that this woman, despite trying to recapture her youth, remembers her responsibilities at home.

111 Aloof and Wearing Makeup

Aloof and wearing makeup
her eyebrows pinched and the thinnest of smiles
her silk dress clinging in the softest of breezes
her cloudlike hair with fake kingfisher curls

Trees in South Garden blooming in spring warmth
pink scented paths littered with elm coins
about to ride the swing she hesitates
worried it's late she goes home

112 七十古來稀

七十古來稀，人人都道。
不是陰功怎生到。
松姿雖瘦，偏耐雪寒霜曉。
看君雙鬢底，青青好。

樓雪初晴，庭闈嬉笑。
一醉何妨玉壺倒。
從今康健，不用靈丹仙草。
更看一百歲，人難老。

Undated and written to the tune "Grateful for Royal Kindness," with the note: "Birthday wishes for Deputy Fan" 壽範倅. Xin Qiji wrote an earlier poem (number 13) to this man who was his deputy in Chuzhou in 1172. This poem was most likely written several decades later, probably in Shangrao in the 1190s.

112 Seventy-Year-Olds Are Rare

Seventy-year-olds are rare
or so people say
it depends on good deeds nobody sees
pine trees might be thin
but they can weather snow and frosty dawns
look at your temples
they're still black

With your roof finally free of ice
and your home full of laughter
why not pour your best when you drink
let your good health begin today
you don't need a pill or magic plant
you'll still see a hundred
and barely feel old

113 江搖病眼昏如霧

江搖病眼昏如霧。
送愁直到津頭路。
歸念樂天詩。
人生足別離。

雲屏深夜語。
夢到君知否。
玉著莫偷垂。
斷腸天下知。

Undated and written to the tune "Bodhisattva Barbarian." Xin Qiji half-heartedly cites cataracts and blurry vision due to sitting in a rocking boat to distract us from the real reason for his tears. Bai Juyi 白居易 (d. 846) was one of the most famous poets of the Tang dynasty. The quoted line was from "Invitation to Drink" 勸酒, a poem Bai wrote seeing off his friend Yu Wuling 于武陵: "Inviting you to raise your golden goblet / I don't need to fill it with words / flowers bloom in the wind and rain / life is full of partings" 勸君金屈卮, 滿酌不須辭. 花發多風雨, 人生足別離. Some sources attribute the poem to Yu Wuling. Room screens of the rich sometimes included sheets of mica in place of paper.

113 Cataract Eyes Bleary from the Waves

Cataract eyes bleary from the waves
seeing you off at the ferry
I recalled Bai Juyi's line
Life is full of partings

We talked all night behind that mica screen
I dreamt of you do you know
I tried to stifle those jade tears
your broken heart was no secret

114 春水

春水，千里，孤舟浪起。
夢攜西子。
覺來村巷夕陽斜。
幾家，短墻紅杏花。

晚雲做造些兒雨。
折花去，岸上誰家女。
太狂顛。
那邊，柳綿，被風吹上天。

Undated and written to the tune "Tang River Story," with the note: "In the Huajian style" 效花間體. The *Huajian Anthology* 花間集 was published in 940 and included the works of eighteen poets who wrote in a romantic style. Xi Shi was one of the famous beauties of ancient China and so distracted the King of Wu, as she was ordered to do, that he lost his kingdom.

114 On a River in Spring

On a river in spring
for a thousand miles
in a sampan on the waves
I dreamt I was holding Xi Shi's hand
I woke as the setting sun lit a village lane
and houses
with short walls and apricot trees in bloom

Evening clouds produced a light rain
on the far shore whose daughter was that
picking flowers
acting crazy
across from me
the willow fuzz
riding the wind to Heaven

115 憶對中秋丹桂叢

憶對中秋丹桂叢。
花在杯中，月在杯中。
今宵樓上一尊同。
雲濕紗窗，雨濕紗窗。

渾欲乘風問化工。
路也難通，信也難通。
滿堂惟有燭花紅。
杯且從容，歌且從容。

Undated and written to the tune "Plum Flower Papercut," with the note: "Mid-Autumn and no moon" 中秋無月. The celebration of the harvest moon is still one of the most important holidays in China. The Chinese see a cassia tree on the moon. The poet's question for Heaven is, "Why no moon tonight?" At the beginning of the second stanza, Xin uses the term *hua-gong* 化工, which means "the operations of nature." It was popular with neo-Confucians when speaking of nature without reifying it. Clearly, though, a reification is what Xin has in mind as he looks up into the sky. Nowadays, *hua-gong* is short for *hua-xue gong-yi* 化学工艺 "chemical engineering."

115 I Recall Mid-Autumn in the Cassia Grove

I recall Mid-Autumn in the cassia grove
the flowers in my cup
the moon in my cup
tonight upstairs the same cup
clouds soaking the window screen
rain soaking the window screen

I wish I could ride the wind and ask Creation
but roads don't go there
and letters don't go there
my room lit only by candlelight
I'm not rushing the cups
I'm not rushing the songs

116 千丈擎天手

千丈擎天手。萬卷懸河口。
黃金腰下印，大如斗。
更千騎弓刀，揮霍遮前後。
百計千方久。
似鬥草兒童，贏個他家偏有。

算枉了，雙眉長恁皺。
白髮空回首。
那時間，說向山中友。
看丘隴牛羊，更辨賢愚否。
且自栽花柳。
怕有人來，但只道，今朝中酒。

Undated and written to the tune "A Single Flower," with the note: "Written for fun while drunk" 醉中戲作.

116 His Strength Supports the Sky

His strength supports the sky
his essays are a waterfall of words
at his waist hangs a seal of gold
big as a dipper
hundreds of armed riders
clear the way in front and behind
his plans and schemes are endless
like the string games children play
to exploit another's weakness

What a waste
his furrowed brows
his white hair recalling the past in vain
on such occasions
he says to his mountain friends
Look at your goats among the graves
can they tell a fool's from a sage's
I'm still planting willows and flowers
but in case he comes here
just say
I'm drinking today

117 金谷無煙宮樹綠

金谷無煙宮樹綠，嫩寒生怕春風。
博山微透暖薰籠。
小樓春色裡，幽夢雨聲中。

別浦鯉魚何封恨重重。
海棠花下去年逢。
也應隨分瘦，忍淚覓殘紅。

Undated and written to the tune "Immortal by the River." Xin Qiji exaggerates a bit about his garden, likening it to one in the capital. Boshan censers—not named for the mountain east of Shangrao—were usually made of copper and shaped like a mountain; inside, one placed small sticks or powder of sandalwood or aloeswood. News from friends was often referred to as "carp," struggling upstream, and their letters as "brocade."

117 My Golden Garden Is Free of Mist My Palace Trees Are Green

My golden garden is free of mist my palace trees are green
I hate when spring turns cold again
my Boshan censer spreads so little warmth
my study is surrounded by signs of spring
my dreams by the sound of rain

When will your carp reach the place where we parted
your brocade letter contained so much sadness
since we met below that quince last year
you must be thinner now
I'm holding back the tears while I search for the petals

118 人面不如花面

人面不如花面，花到開時重見。
獨倚小闌干，許多山。

落葉西風時候，人共青山都瘦。
說道夢陽臺，幾曾來。

Undated and written to the tune "Zhaojun's Complaint." Sun Terrace was on Shaman Mountain 巫山, in the first of the Yangzi's Three Gorges. King Huai 楚懷王 of the ancient kingdom of Chu traveled here in a dream and met an immortal maiden.

118 People Faces Aren't like Flower Faces

People faces aren't like flower faces
flowers bloom and we see them again
I lean against the railing alone
the ridges extend forever

When the west wind blows and the leaves fall
people and mountains look thinner
as for dreaming about Sun Terrace
when will that ever happen

119 一片歸心擬亂雲

一片歸心擬亂雲，春來諳盡惡黃昏。
不堪向晚檐前雨，又待今宵滴夢魂。

爐燼冷，鼎香氛，酒寒誰遣為重溫。
何人柳外橫雙笛，客耳那堪不忍聞。

Undated and written to the tune "Partridge Sky." Dusk and late night are when someone far from home is reminded of the distance. The twin, or double, flute is associated with non-Han ethnic groups in China and consists of two resonant bamboo tubes with three holes but different pitches.

119 My Homesick Heart Is like a Swirling Cloud

My homesick heart is like a swirling cloud
dusks have been the worst this spring
unable to endure the rain at dark
I'm expecting it in my dreams again tonight

The stove is cold
just incense smoke
someone forgot to warm the wine
who's that playing a twin flute beyond the willows
how can an exile not listen

120 此生自斷天休問

此生自斷天休問，獨倚危樓。
獨倚危樓，不信人間有別愁。

君來正是眠時節，君且歸休。
君且歸休，說與西風一任秋。

Undated and written to the tune "Ugly Servant." The repeated line in the first stanza is from the poem "Climbing the Xiazhou City Tower" 登夏州城樓 by Luo Yin 羅隱 (d. 909), written upon looking out over an ancient battlefield.

120 About This Life I've Stopped Asking Heaven

About this life I've stopped asking Heaven
standing on a high tower alone
standing on a high tower alone
I doubt anyone is as sad

You came just as I was going to bed
you may as well go home
you may as well go home
tell the autumn wind to go ahead and blow

121 寶釵分

寶釵分，桃葉渡，煙柳暗南浦。
怕上層樓，十日九風雨。
斷腸片片飛紅，都無人管，更誰勸，啼鶯聲住。

鬢邊覷，應把花卜歸期，纔簪又重數。
羅帳燈昏，哽咽夢中語。
是他春帶愁來，春歸何處，卻不解，帶將愁去。

Undated and written to the tune "Zhu Yingtai Prelude," with the note: "Late spring" 晚春. Hairpins in ancient China usually came in pairs—one for each side of the hairdo. It was a custom for a woman to give one to her lover or husband to bring back whenever he left on a journey. Peach Petal Ferry was the frequent scene of parting in Nanjing. The ferry operated where the Qinhuai and Qingxi Rivers 青溪 met. There is still a memorial arch on the north shore and an alley behind it named for the ferry.

121 Since Dividing Her Jeweled Hairpins

Since dividing her jeweled hairpins
at Peach Petal Ferry
on the south shore behind the willows
she's been afraid to go upstairs
ten days and nine with rain
as for the falling pink pieces of her heart
no one cares
much less tells
the orioles to stop singing

Noticing them in her hair
she counts the petals to divine his return
then puts them back and counts them again
in the lantern light behind the silk curtains
she sobs and talks in her sleep
every spring brings sorrows
wherever it is spring goes
it never learns
to take them away

122 溪邊白鷺

溪邊白鷺。
來我告洳。
溪裡魚兒堪數。
主人憐汝汝憐魚，要物我欣然一處。

白沙遠浦。
青泥別渚。
剩有蝦跳鰍舞。
聽君飛去飽時來，看頭上風吹一縷。

Undated and written to the tune "Magpie Bridge Immortal," with the note: "For an egret" 贈鷺鷥.

122 Egret by the Shore

Egret by the shore
I have something to say
concerning the number of fish in the river
I love you and you love fish
and I want us both to be happy

By the distant delta's shimmering sand
there's a shoal of the blackest mud
shrimp are jumping and loaches dancing
why not fly there and eat your fill
let's see that plume on your head in the wind

123 世事從頭減

世事從頭減，秋懷徹底清。
夜深猶送枕邊聲，試問清溪底事未能平。

月到愁邊白，雞先遠處鳴。
是中無有利和名，因甚山前未曉有人行。

Undated and written to the tune "Southern Song," with the note: "Spending a night in the mountains" 山中夜坐.

123 Worldly Concerns Are Waning Again

Worldly concerns are waning again
the longings of fall are increasingly clear
when late-night sounds still reach my pillow
I ask the stream if it can't quiet down

The moon looks brighter to those who are sad
the first rooster is always the one farthest away
if profit and fame mean nothing here
why are people on the road before dawn lights the hills

124 僧窗夜雨

僧窗夜雨，茶鼎熏爐宜小住。
却恨春風，勾引詩來惱殺翁。

狂歌未可，且把一尊料理我。
我到亡何，却聽儂家陌上歌。

Undated and written to the tune "Magnolia Flower—Short Version," with the note: "While spending a night at a monastery" 宿僧房有作. Buddhist monasteries often provided spartan lodging to men of status who found themselves on the road at night. A small tea stove and incense censer, as well as a wineskin, were typical travel gear for such men. Xin's wineskin was just the thing for such a night—even in a monastery. I kept a bottle of cream sherry in my room at the monastery in Taiwan and when the moon was full often found myself on the building's flat roof.

124 Night Rain on the Monastery Window

Night rain on the monastery window
my tea stove and censer unpacked
how I hate spring weather
the poems it stirs trouble an old man

Since singing isn't allowed
I enjoyed some wine
until I had no choice
out on the road I let my voice go

125 青山非不佳

青山非不佳，未解留儂住。
赤腳踏層冰，為愛清溪故。

朝來山鳥啼，勸上山高處。
我意不關渠，自要尋蘭去。

Undated and written to the tune "Fresh Hawthorn Berries," with the note: "Hiking alone on West Cliff" 獨遊西巖. This cliff was on Boshan, east of Shangrao.

125 Not That Mountains Aren't Fine

Not that mountains aren't fine
but they've never held my attention
I walk on the ice barefoot
because I love crystalline streams

Birds were calling this morning
urging me to climb the peak
I ignored them on purpose
I was planning to look for orchids

126 去年燕子來

去年燕子來，繡戶深深處。
花徑得泥歸，都把琴書污。

今年燕子來，誰聽呢喃語。
不見捲簾人，一陣黃昏雨。

Undated and written to the tune "Fresh Hawthorn Berries," with the note: "Someone asked for a poem, and I wrote this for them" 有覓詞者, 為賦. Recessed quarters were those where women lived.

126 Last Year When the Swallows Came

Last year when the swallows came
to recessed embroidered quarters
bringing mud from flower-lined paths
my books and zither suffered

This year when the swallows came
I heard no twittering talk
or saw anyone raise a curtain
nothing but rain at dusk

Xin Qiji died on the third day of the tenth month of 1207. He was buried here on Yangyuan Hill 陽源山, six kilometers west of his home at Piaoquan Spring. The home is long gone, but the spring is still there, on the west side of what is now Highway G237. Across the road is Qisi Ford 期思渡, the former location of Camphor Tree Bridge. (Photo by Bill Porter.)

Xin Qiji Timeline

1140 born in Jinan

1148 father dies; moves to Bozhou

1148–1158 raised by grandfather Xin Zan

1159 grandfather dies; mourning period begins

1161 mourning period ends; raises two-thousand-man force; joins Geng Jing's army

1162 audience with Emperor Gaozong; joins his ten-thousand-man army with Song forces

1163 settles in Zhenjiang; marries; builds house

1164–1177 serves in Jiangyin, Nanjing, Chuzhou, Changsha, and Nanchang

1178–1180 begins building Daihu Lake house; serves at court in Hangzhou

1181 forced to resign; moves to Shangrao

1186 buys Piaoquan Spring property near Yanshan

1188 publishes his first collection of poems

1192–1194 accepts temporary assignment in Fuzhou

1195 Daihu Lake house burns; relocates to Piaoquan Spring

1203 helps Han Tuozhou with war plans

1204–1205 at Emperor Ningzong's request, serves as magistrate of Zhenjiang

1207 dies at Piaoquan Spring

About the Chinese Text

The first edition of Xin Qiji's work, The Lyric Poems of Jiaxuan 稼軒詞, was published by his friend Fan Kai 范開 in the first month of 1188, when Xin was forty-nine. There are no extant copies of that first printing, nor are there extant copies of the subsequent three printings to which additional poems were added. We do, however, have copies from a later Southern Song printing of all four—汲古閣影宋鈔本. A separate twelve-folio edition of his work, titled The Lyrics of Jiaxuan 稼軒長短句, was also published during the Southern Song, sometime after his death. Although no copies of that edition's original printing exist, we have reprints based on a copy preserved in the Siyinzhai 四印齋刻本 collection of ancient texts. In preparing my translations of the poems, and in choosing among variants and deciding on dates, I have consulted both editions as well as the works below.

Commentaries and Studies

English-language study of Xin Qiji's life and poems: *Hsin Ch'i-chi* by Irving Yucheng Lo, published in 1971 by Twayne, Woodbridge, Connecticut. LOC Catalog: 70-120509

Critical edition of Xin Qiji's extant lyric poems 稼軒詞編年箋注 edited by Deng Guangming 鄧廣銘, published in 2018 by 上海古籍出版社, Shanghai, China. ISBN: 978-7-532-58745-2

Biography and chronology of Xin Qiji's life and works 辛弃疾传, 辛弃疾年 by Deng Guangming 邓广铭, published in 2017 by 新知三联书店, Beijing, China. ISBN: 978-7-108-05885-0

Chinese Commentaries on Selected Lyric Poems

辛弃疾词选 by Liu Yangzhong 刘扬忠, published in 2021 by 人民文学出版社, Beijing, China. ISBN: 978-7-020-17027-2

辛棄疾詞精選 by Sun Yanwen 孫燕文, published in 2017 by 文國書局, Tainan, Taiwan. ISBN: 978-986-247-167-8

新譯辛棄疾詞 by Nie Anfu 聶安福, published in 2015 by 三民書局, Taipei, Taiwan. ISBN: 978-957-14-6005-5

Study of poems written on Boshan 辛弃疾在博 by Li Youxiang 李有祥, published in 2023 by江西人民出版社, Nanchang, China. ISBN: 978-7-210-13171-7

Study of Xin Qiji's life and poems, focused on his time in Shangrao and Yanshan 辛弃疾信州词与信州生 by Jijun 汲军 and Ying Zikang 应子康, published in 2010 by 光明日报出版社, Beijing, China. ISBN: 978-7-802-06564-2

Index of Tune Titles

Identified by poem number

About Red Pine

Bill Porter assumes the pen name Red Pine for his translation work. He was born in Los Angeles in 1943, grew up in the Idaho Panhandle, served a tour of duty in the US Army, graduated from the University of California with a degree in anthropology, and attended graduate school at Columbia University. Uninspired by the prospect of an academic career, he dropped out of Columbia and moved to a Buddhist monastery in Taiwan. After more than three years with the monks and nuns, he struck out on his own and supported himself by teaching English and later by working as a journalist at English-language radio stations in Taiwan and Hong Kong. Having spent twenty-two years in Asia, Porter returned to the US in 1993 and has lived ever since in Port Townsend, Washington. His poetry translations have been honored with a number of awards, including two NEA translation fellowships, a Guggenheim Fellowship, a PEN Translation Prize, and the inaugural Asian Literature Award of the American Literary Translators Association. Porter also received the 2018 Thornton Wilder Prize for Translation bestowed by the American Academy of Arts and Letters, and in 2023, he was honored with China's top publishing prize for foreigners, the Special Book Award of China, for *Finding Them Gone: Visiting China's Poets of the Past* (2016).

Poets for Poetry

Copper Canyon Press poets are at the center of all our efforts as a nonprofit publisher. Poets not only create the art that defines our books, but they read and teach the books we publish. Many are also generous donors who believe in financially supporting the larger poetry community of Copper Canyon Press. For decades, our poets have quietly donated their royalties, have directly engaged in our fundraising campaigns, and have made personal donations in support of the next generation. Their support has encouraged the innovative risk-taking that sustains and furthers the art form.

The donor-poets who have contributed to the Press since 2023 include:

Jonathan Aaron
Kelli Russell Agodon
Pamela Alexander
Joyce Harrington Bahle
Ellen Bass
Mark Bibbins
Sherwin Bitsui
Marianne Boruch
Laure-Anne Bosselaar
Cyrus Cassells
Peter Cole and Adina Hoffman
Elizabeth J. Coleman
John Freeman
Forrest Gander
Jenny George
Daniel Gerber
Julian Gewirtz
Jorie Graham
Robert and Carolyn Hedin
Bob Hicok
Ha Jin
Jaan Kaplinski
Laura Kasischke
Jennifer L. Knox
Ted Kooser
Deborah Landau
Sung-Il Lee
Ben Lerner
Dana Levin
Heather McHugh
Jane Miller
Lisa Olstein
Gregory Orr
Eric Pankey
Kevin Prufer
Paisley Rekdal
James Richardson
Alberto Ríos
David Romtvedt
Natalie Shapero
Arthur Sze
Elaine Terranova
Chase Twichell
Ocean Vuong
Connie Wanek-Dentinger
Emily Warn

Poetry is vital to language and living. Since 1972, Copper Canyon Press has published extraordinary poetry from around the world to engage the imaginations and intellects of readers, writers, booksellers, librarians, teachers, students, and donors.

We are grateful for the major support provided by:

academy of american poets

A& OFFICE OF ARTS & CULTURE SEATTLE

ARTSFUND

THE PAUL G. ALLEN FAMILY FOUNDATION

Hawthornden Foundation

POETRY FOUNDATION

INGRAM CONTENT GROUP

the point envision · enact · evolve

McSWEENEY'S

WASHINGTON STATE ARTS COMMISSION

ART WORKS. National Endowment for the Arts arts.gov

The Witter Bynner Foundation for Poetry

TO LEARN MORE ABOUT UNDERWRITING
COPPER CANYON PRESS TITLES,
PLEASE CALL 360-385-4925 EXT. 105

WE ARE GRATEFUL FOR THE MAJOR SUPPORT PROVIDED BY:

Anonymous
Jill Baker and Jeffrey Bishop
Anne and Geoffrey Barker
Donna Bellew
Lisha Bian
Will Blythe
John Branch
Diana Broze
John R. Cahill
Sarah J. Cavanaugh
Keith Cowan and Linda Walsh
Peter Currie
Geralyn White Dreyfous
The Evans Family
Mimi Gardner Gates
Gull Industries Inc.
  on behalf of William True
Carolyn and Robert Hedin
David and Jane Hibbard
Bruce S. Kahn
Phil Kovacevich and Eric Wechsler
Maureen Lee and Mark Busto
Ellie Mathews and Carl Youngmann
  as The North Press
Larry Mawby and Lois Bahle
Petunia Charitable Fund and
  adviser Elizabeth Hebert
Suzanne Rapp and Mark Hamilton
Adam and Lynn Rauch
Emily and Dan Raymond
Joseph C. Roberts
Cynthia Sears
Kim and Jeff Seely
Tree Swenson
Julia Sze
Barbara and Charles Wright
In honor of C.D. Wright
  from Forrest Gander
Caleb Young as C. Young Creative
The dedicated interns and faithful
  volunteers of Copper Canyon Press

The pressmark for Copper Canyon Press
suggests entrance, connection, and interaction
while holding at its center
an attentive, dynamic space for poetry.

This book is set in Adobe Garamond Pro.
Book design by Gopa & Ted2, Inc.
Printed on archival-quality paper.